W9-BLB-823

"Rich with tools, examples, and practical advice"

Praise for *Strengthening Nonprofit Performance*

"This is a great book! The authors have taken the unwieldy topic of capacity building and distilled it into understandable implications and strategic choices for any reader interested in building the strength of the nonprofit sector. The theoretical framework is sound, and the suggested approaches for programmatic application are practical and well tested. I expect this book to become a key resource for the whole field, not only the foundation community. The book is very well organized and a thorough and current treatment of the topic. I think the practical, yet still concise, guidance to defining capacity building, looking at options for an individual foundation, cautions (such as the three-way relationship among funders, providers, and nonprofits), and emphasis on values are all very helpful."

Mike Allison, Director, Consulting and Research Group, CompassPoint Nonprofit Services, San Francisco

"There's something for every grantmaker in *Strengthening Nonprofit Performance*. The authors provide a real road map to help any type of funder get an effort to support organizational effectiveness off the ground. Rich with tools, examples and practical advice, this book adds real value to our field."

Kathleen P. Enright, Executive Director, Grantmakers for Effective Organizations, Washington, DC

"Effective service to society demands excellence in performance from nonprofit organizations and the funders that support them. Connolly and Lukas provide funders with insight and practical guidance to build capacity within their own organizations and within the organizations they serve."

Rob Johnston, President and CEO, Peter F. Drucker Foundation for Nonprofit Management, New York City

"Connolly and Lukas present a practical work on the complex subject of capacity building—its practice, funding, and evaluation—in easy-to-follow terms that philanthropists, consultants, and nonprofit managers alike will find useful in both their day-to-day work and in strategizing for the future."

Deborah Linnell, Linnell & Associates, Wickford, Rhode Island

"A welcome addition to the growing literature on the management of nonprofit organizations. Marrying practical advice with clearly explicated discussions of the academic and research literature, this book will prove valuable to practitioners and academics alike."

Sharon Oster, Frederick D. Wolfe Professor of Management and Entrepreneurship, Yale School of Management, New Haven, and author, Strategic Management for Nonprofit Organizations

A FUNDER'S GUIDE
from **WILDER & GEO**

Strengthening Nonprofit Performance: A Funder's Guide to Capacity Building is one of a series of works published by Amherst H. Wilder Foundation in collaboration with Grantmakers for Effective Organizations (GEO). Together, we hope to strengthen nonprofit organizations, the communities they serve, and the nonprofit sector by helping grantmakers in their work with nonprofits.

Strengthening Nonprofit Performance:
A Funder's Guide to Capacity Building

by Paul Connolly and Carol Lukas

Strengthening Nonprofit Performance:
A Funder's Guide to Capacity Building

by Paul Connolly and Carol Lukas

AMHERST H.
WILDER
FOUNDATION

SAINT PAUL,
MINNESOTA

We thank The David and Lucile Packard Foundation and the Amherst H. Wilder Foundation
for support of this publication.

The Amherst H. Wilder Foundation is one of the largest and oldest endowed human service and community development organizations in the United States. Since 1906, the Wilder Foundation has been providing health and human services that help children and families grow strong, the elderly age with dignity, and the community grow in its ability to meet its own needs.

We hope you find this book helpful! Should you need additional information about our services, please contact:

Wilder Center for Communities
Amherst H. Wilder Foundation
919 Lafond Avenue
Saint Paul, MN 55104
(651) 642-4022

For more information about other Wilder Foundation publications, please see the back of this book or contact:

Wilder Publishing Center
Amherst H. Wilder Foundation
919 Lafond Avenue
Saint Paul, MN 55104
(800) 274-6024
www.wilder.org/pubs

To learn more about TCC Group, contact:

The TCC Group
50 East 42nd Street, 19th Floor
New York, NY 10017
(212) 949-0990
www.tccgrp.com

Edited by Vincent Hyman

Book design by Mighty Media, Minneapolis, MN
    Text: Chris Long
    Charts: Kelly Doudna

Cover illustration: Rebecca Andrews

Manufactured in the United States of America

Second printing, August 2004

Library of Congress Cataloging-in-Publication Data

Connolly, Paul, 1962–

   Strengthening nonprofit performance : a funder's guide to capacity building / by Paul Connolly and Carol Lukas.

      p.   cm.

Includes bibliographical references and index.

   ISBN 0-940069-37-7 (pbk.)

1. Nonprofit organizations--Management. I. Lukas, Carol A., 1947– II. Title.

   HD62.6 .C664 2002

   361.7'632'068--dc21

                                                              2002013832

Printed on recycled paper. 10 percent postconsumer waste

About the Authors

PAUL CONNOLLY is senior vice president at TCC Group (formerly The Conservation Company), a twenty-three-year-old firm with offices in New York and Philadelphia and full-time staff based in Chicago and San Francisco. He leads the firm's nonprofit practice and serves on its board of directors. TCC Group provides management consulting, strategic planning, and evaluation services to nonprofit organizations, private foundations, and corporate citizenship programs. The firm has assisted a variety of funders to plan, implement, and evaluate capacity building activities, including the Ford Foundation, the Hartford Foundation for Public Giving, the William and Flora Hewlett Foundation, the James Irvine Foundation, Massachusetts Cultural Council, New York City HIV Health and Human Services Planning Council, the New York Community Trust, the David and Lucile Packard Foundation, Pfizer, Inc., the William Penn Foundation, the Robin Hood Foundation, UBS Paine Webber, and the United Way of New York City.

Paul provides consulting services to nonprofits and grantmakers and serves on several nonprofit boards. He has published articles and conducted numerous workshops related to nonprofit management and capacity building. He is co-author of *Increasing Cultural Participation: An Audience Development Planning Handbook for Presenters, Producers, and Their Collaborators*. Paul received a master of arts degree in public and private management from Yale University School of Management and a bachelor of arts degree from Harvard University.

Paul Connolly can be reached at TCC Group, 50 East 42nd Street, 19th Floor, New York, NY 10017, 212-949-0990 ext. 218, pconnolly@tccgrp.com.

CAROL LUKAS is director of National Services for the Wilder Center for Communities at the Amherst H. Wilder Foundation in St. Paul, Minnesota. Wilder Center for Communities (WCC) provides a broad range of research, consulting, training, and publishing services to nonprofits and communities, and serves as partner and coordinator for local and national capacity building initiatives. WCC has assisted many funders and national organizations in planning and implementing capacity building efforts, including Council of Leadership Foundations, Grantmakers for Effective Organizations, Indiana University Center on Philanthropy, Habitat for Humanity International, the Pew Charitable Trusts, the David and Lucile Packard Foundation, Minnesota Council on Foundations, the Saint Paul Foundation, United Way of America, Blandin Foundation, and Howard Heinz Endowment.

Carol has over twenty-five years of consulting and training experience with nonprofit, government, community, and private sector organizations. She has worked with large networks, alliances, communities, and nonprofit capacity building efforts. Carol is author of *Consulting with Nonprofits: A Practitioners Guide* and co-author of *Community Forums: Engaging Citizens, Mobilizing Communities,* both published by Amherst H. Wilder Foundation. She has degrees in urban planning and organization development.

Carol Lukas can be reached at: Wilder Center for Communities, 919 Lafond Avenue, St. Paul, MN 55104, (651) 642-2024, cal@wilder.org.

Acknowledgments

Paul Connolly and Carol Lukas thank the people who helped during the writing of this book by providing guidance, sharing their grantmaking experience, and reviewing the manuscript:

Mike Allison	Richard Mittenthal
Bryan Barry	Ruth Norris
Marty Campbell	Michael Park
Jim Canales	Michael Seltzer
A. Scott Dupree	Paul Shoemaker
Mary Ann Holohean	John Tomlinson
Barbara Kibbe	Gayle Williams
Deb Linnell	Peter York
Paul Mattessich	

We thank all of the grantmakers and researchers whose work we cite as examples—the list is too long for individual names. They have contributed mightily to the building of this field, and their stories will guide others venturing into the world of capacity building.

We thank the Wilder Publishing Center staff—Becky Andrews, Kirsten Nielsen, and especially Vince Hyman—for their wisdom, patience, and exceptional guidance during book development.

We thank the David and Lucile Packard Foundation for its funding and support of this book. And we are grateful to Grantmakers for Effective Organizations (GEO) for sponsoring the first workshop on this material and allowing us to get early reactions from an audience of grantmakers.

Paul Connolly is especially thankful for his colleagues at TCC Group who contributed to the creation of this publication, including John Riggan,

Richard Mittenthal, Shelly Kessler, Peter York (who provided significant input to the section on evaluation), Laura Colin Klein, Anne Sherman, Hydie Miller, Christine Korinedes, Kitty Barnes, and Melissa Knott. He appreciates his clients who shared their wisdom with him over the years and helped inform his contribution to this book. He owes a special debt to Dana Blackburn, Dianne Mead, and especially Lloyd Cheu for their support while he was writing this book. Finally, he is grateful to his parents, Joe and Ann Connolly, who taught him the importance of public and voluntary service and giving back to the community.

Carol Lukas is grateful for the support and encouragement of her colleagues at Wilder Center for Communities—Bryan Barry for his insight and suggestions, Angela Ryan for her tireless research and support, Paul Fate and Carol Zapfel for their patience and help with her day job, and Emil Angelica, Linda Hoskins, and Maricarmen Cortes for their encouragement. She thanks the many nonprofit and community leaders who have been her teachers. And she thanks Brenna Barrett and Christopher Barrett for helping her believe she knows things worth writing about.

Contents

Introduction

The Growing Interest in Building Organizational Capacity

S OCIETY TODAY RELIES MORE AND MORE ON NONPROFIT OR-
ganizations to provide critical services, advocate for public policy,
and stimulate innovation. As a result, funders and nonprofits share
two common concerns: how to make better use of limited resources in the
face of growing need, and how to achieve important outcomes in a vola-
tile, changing environment. Increasingly, funders and nonprofits alike are
turning to the same strategy to address these concerns: improving organizational effectiveness.

"Let's start with an assumption: that a nonprofit organization is more
likely to reach its programmatic goals if it is well managed," says Barbara
Kibbe, program director, Organizational Effectiveness, at the David and
Lucile Packard Foundation. "That assumption is the foundation of our
Organizational Effectiveness Program."[1] Although the foundation has sup-
ported capacity building among its grantees since 1983, its Organizational
Effectiveness Program has grown significantly in the last five years and has
expanded to include building the field of nonprofit management.

A rising number of private and corporate funders are committed to building
effective nonprofit organizations that have the capacity to create and sustain high-impact programs. And the levels of funding for capacity building

are increasing. A quick review of Foundation Center data illustrates this growing commitment. Between 1989 and 1999, technical assistance grants increased 125 percent, to $135 million. Grants for management development rose 124 percent, to $159 million, between 1994 and 1999.

Trustees, donors, and regulators are demanding greater accountability from nonprofits financially and programmatically, resulting in increased attention not only to *what* nonprofits do, but also to *how* they do it. An increasing number of funders are practicing a more engaged style of grantmaking and expect a greater return on their investment. Many philanthropists are also demanding greater attention to organizational effectiveness.

Over the past several years, a critical mass of funders interested in organizational effectiveness has emerged, leading to a more disciplined study of the field, and a broader community of practice. Grantmakers for Effective Organizations, an affinity group of the Council on Foundations, formed only a few years ago, now has over five hundred members. Other funder networks—including Grantmakers Evaluation Network, Grantmakers in Health, Grantmakers in the Arts, and regional associations of grantmakers—offer programs related to organizational capacity building.

The Origins of This Book

We wrote this book because more funders are actively supporting capacity building efforts, and even more are wanting to begin, yet don't know where or how to get the information they need. We've tried to bring together in one place answers to many of the questions funders are asking about the complex and evolving field of nonprofit capacity building, including *What is it? Why is it important? How do I start? Who else is doing it? What are the different approaches I can use? How do I know if our efforts are achieving results?*

We chose to work together on this book because we thought that the reader would benefit from our collective thirty-five-plus years of complementary experience working with various types of funders, capacity builders, and nonprofits. As we wrote the book, we learned a lot from each other. We agreed on most subjects, but had lively debates about others. In most cases, we ended up sharing the same perspective. In a few cases, we agreed to disagree and included alternative approaches in the book. Some of the more difficult debates include *Who decides what kind of capacity needs to be built? What kinds of capacity building interventions get the best results? Should funders be the direct providers of capacity building services?* We also found that as hard as we tried to avoid jargon, the book is full of terms that are used a lot and rarely defined. The worst culprit in this category is the term *capacity building*.* (In Chapter 2 we propose a way of thinking about capacity building that helps define the concept.)

This book provides a scan of the many strategies that grantmakers can use to build the capacity of nonprofit organizations and communities, with examples of strategies employed by various grantmakers. At the present time, little conclusive research exists on which strategies are more effective than others. We encourage readers to contact other grantmakers, to research the success of various strategies, and to adapt promising strategies to fit their situation.

Capacity building presents exciting challenges. To help meet them, nonprofits, funders, and providers need to make better use of research to answer the more perplexing questions about capacity building. Those involved need to study lessons from other sectors, yet understand the unique conditions affecting nonprofits. And everyone needs to listen well and continue to advance a common understanding of how to strengthen and sustain nonprofits to tackle the huge needs in our communities.

We hope this book contributes to the conversation and stimulates dialogue on the topic of capacity building.

* "Capacity" and "capacity building" are imperfect terms that can be vague buzzwords (see Tony Proscio's "In Other Words: A Plea for Plain Speaking in Foundations," a booklet published in 2000 by the Edna McConnell Clark Foundation.) In this section, we try to define these words clearly. In other parts of the book, we sometimes use these terms, and when possible, use more specific words.

How to Use This Book

We wrote this book to help you and your organization decide whether and how to support nonprofit capacity building efforts. Knowing that readers will have different levels of interest and various needs for tools, we organized the book to make it simple to read either for a quick scan of current thinking or for more in-depth, how-to ideas.

The book is organized into five sections:

Chapter 1: Why Invest in Capacity Building suggests compelling reasons for funders to commit resources to capacity building.

Chapter 2: What Capacity Building Is defines capacity and capacity building, examines the components of organizational capacity in more depth, and describes types of capacity building activities. It also describes the role of capacity building providers.

Chapter 3: How to Build the Capacity of Nonprofits describes general guidelines for funders supporting capacity building. The reader then follows a flexible four-step process for developing and implementing a capacity building strategy and plan.

> **Step 1: Plan to Plan** helps you create a planning process that will result in a solid plan.

> **Step 2: Take Stock** includes assessing your own organization's readiness and capabilities for starting a capacity building effort, reviewing needs and opportunities in the community, and identifying your organization's values.

> **Step 3: Set Direction** involves establishing goals and objectives, selecting capacity building strategies, and committing resources.

> **Step 4: Take Action and Evaluate** covers implementation and evaluation approaches and tools.

4

Chapter 4: Capacity Building Strategies describes a range of approaches funders can use to strengthen nonprofit organizations and gives examples of how each approach has been used in different settings.

The **Appendices** include capacity building tips for funders whose reach extends beyond the United States; listings of publications, web sites, and organizations providing information about capacity building; and blank worksheets for planning, implementing, and evaluating capacity building efforts. You may reproduce these worksheets as needed to facilitate your planning. Worksheets are also available online to purchasers of this book. To use the online worksheets, visit the following web address:

http://www.wilder.org/pubs/workshts/pubs_worksheets1.html?377shp

Who Can Benefit from This Book

This book is written for all types of funders, including community, independent, public, family, or corporate foundations; corporate giving programs; federated giving organizations; or government agencies. It can be beneficial whether you focus exclusively on capacity building efforts or work in other program areas; work at a small or large organization; are a staff member or trustee of a grantmaking organization; are a venture philanthropist or a traditional funder; or fund locally or internationally. Those who provide capacity building assistance to nonprofits, as well as staff and trustees of nonprofit organizations, may also find the book beneficial.

Different types of readers might want to use the book in various ways.

- If you are inexperienced in building nonprofit organizational capacity, you might want to read the whole book to get a comprehensive orientation to the topic.
- If you are experienced in capacity building work, you could read specific sections to learn more about new approaches, what other funders are doing, or how to evaluate capacity building.

- If you work at a small funding organization with limited financial and human resources or are just beginning and want to start small, you might want to follow a streamlined planning process (see the "shortcut" sidebars in Chapter 3) and concentrate on the low-cost strategies described in Chapter 4.

- If you work at a large funding organization or want to develop a major, comprehensive capacity building initiative, you could follow the more deliberate planning process described in Chapter 3 and consider a range of strategies with varying costs.

- If you are a venture philanthropist, you might want to focus on the Lessons Learned section in Chapter 3 and the direct management assistance strategy in Chapter 4.

- If you are interested in building the capacity of nongovernmental organizations in countries outside the United States, be sure to read Appendix A.

- If you work for a government agency, you will note that the book provides only a few examples of public agencies. However, many of the concepts and approaches described are applicable for government agencies.

- If you are a capacity building provider, or a staff member or trustee of a nonprofit organization, you can review the book for a comprehensive description of the field and the variety of grantmaking strategies. The guidelines in the Lessons Learned section of Chapter 3 will further your understanding of the relationships among funders, capacity builders, and nonprofits.

The capacity building strategies and processes described in this book can be adapted to fit the goals, size, and means of many kinds of funding organizations. We hope you find it valuable as your organization begins or expands its work to improve the effectiveness of nonprofit organizations.

Chapter 1

Why Invest in Capacity Building

T HE TERM *CAPACITY BUILDING* REFERS TO THE process of strengthening an organization in order to improve its performance and impact. Capacity building has long been an integral aspect of for-profit business practices. Private sector investors look for organizations that have strong leadership, management systems, and infrastructure. Yet historically, most investors in the nonprofit sector—funders—have focused almost exclusively on programs.

This chapter provides an historical overview of funders' support for capacity building, and it outlines the main reasons funders are, in growing numbers, investing in capacity building efforts.

Although funders' interest in strengthening the capacity of nonprofit organizations is growing, it is not new. For several decades, local and national foundations in many parts of the country have earmarked grants for management and technical assistance for nonprofit groups. Despite such efforts, many of the fundamental challenges associated with nonprofit management and governance remain the same. Most nonprofits still do not pay enough attention to management concerns. Many large national foundations continue to limit funding to special programs and short-term projects, often creating disincentives to good management, rather than supporting the organizational capacity building that nonprofits need. Many funders still believe that funding core organizational infrastructure diverts money from those who directly benefit from program services.

Reasons to Invest in Capacity Building

Funders that invest in building the capacity of nonprofit organizations do so for three main reasons. Capacity building can

1. Enhance program impact

2. Increase nonprofit and community sustainability

3. Leverage philanthropic dollars

Enhance program impact

Many factors can limit nonprofit program impact. The program may serve a compelling unmet need but lack the leadership or organizational infrastructure to address it effectively. The program may be artfully designed and achieve great outcomes but may not be implemented at a large enough scale. A group may have an exciting program model but cannot demonstrate whether it is achieving the desired outcomes. Or an organization may historically have delivered quality programs but finds itself unable to revamp its operations quickly enough to stay effective in the face of changing demographics and labor shortages. Many of the commonly understood methods of strengthening program effectiveness and reach—evaluating and redesigning programs, bringing successful pilot efforts to scale, spurring replication, and furthering in-depth partnerships and collaborations—all require capacity building support, just as a growing private company requires working capital.

As a funder, you may ask yourself, Why support a program if the organization is not run well? You might believe that strong organizations lead to strong programs, that organizations are far more likely to reach their programmatic goals if they are well managed. By increasing the capability of nonprofit organizations to produce desired outcomes, you can minimize risk, make longer-term investments in grantees, and help them to better help the clients and communities they serve. McKinsey & Company notes in a report on capacity building, prepared for Venture Philanthropy Partners, that "although the link between increased capacity and increased impact may be hard to quantify, one does lead to the other."[2]

Increase nonprofit and community sustainability

The accelerating rate of change and major restructuring of the nonprofit sector are taking a toll on nonprofit organizations. The distinctions between for-profit, nonprofit, and public sectors are blurring as each sector adapts new approaches and vehicles from the other. Competition among sectors is heightened as managed health care expands, education becomes more privatized, and government outsourcing grows. Stakeholders are calling for more value and accountability from nonprofits. The population is becoming more diverse. Rapid technological progress has allowed larger, well-financed nonprofits to automate, streamline operations, and take advantage of more affordable and efficient telecommunications, while smaller nonprofits, often serving the most pressing social needs, have not been able to do so. The sidebar A Sampling of Trends Affecting Nonprofits on page 10 provides more detail on these trends.

Change is constant and evolution is imperative for nonprofits. Successful organizations must continually adapt and strengthen their capacity to survive and fulfill their mission. And, they must become ever-more agile as they strive to provide quality programs to diverse constituents. In this rapidly changing and highly competitive environment, it is harder for nonprofit organizations to sustain themselves and survive. Capacity building is needed to help nonprofits constantly scan their environment; stay on top of changing social, economic, and industry trends; and keep their organization healthy and viable.

Frazierita Klasen, assistant director for Local Programs at the Pew Charitable Trusts, explains why the Trusts have recently expanded support for organizational effectiveness: "Pew has always funded services, and that will continue to be our primary work. But now we've made additional resources available to help nonprofit organizations respond to the tremendous changes in their operating environment. It gives these agencies an opportunity to do some thoughtful planning and analysis to improve their capacity. And to do these things without compromising programs while they shore up infrastructure."[3]

Funders may also see organizational capacity building as a way to help strengthen individuals, communities, and civil society.* Human capital is

> * Civil society is a sphere of ideas, values, institutions, organizations, networks, and individuals located between the family, the state, and the market that help to spread democracy and encourage development.

A Sampling of Trends Affecting Nonprofits

Political and Regulatory Trends

- Government, business, and nonprofits engage in activities traditionally limited to other sectors; competition between sectors increases

- Government provides fewer direct services, relies more on other sectors

- Managed care model from health sector extends to human services

- Public increasingly demands value and accountability from nonprofits

Social and Demographic Trends

- Income disparity between high- and low-income people widens

- Cultural and ethnic diversity increases

- "Graying of the population" continues

- Social and economic position of women continues to change

- Nontraditional families increase

Economic Trends

- Individual giving grows as wealth transfers from one generation to another

- Turbulent economy leads to fluctuating foundation asset levels and giving patterns and causes financial uncertainty for nonprofits

- Corporate contributions and community involvement become more linked to business activity

- The gap between nonprofit and corporate pay scales widens

Technological Trends

- More organizational functions become automated

- Telecommunications and information management systems become easier to use, more affordable, and more efficient

- Access to information increases as technology becomes more prevalent

- Gap widens between those with and without technology

at the core of every organization, and the individuals who work or volunteer in the organization need to change in order for organizations to change. When nonprofit organizations become more effective, communities and the people the nonprofits serve benefit more. Consultant Ann Philbin writes that "an organization's level of accountability to its community, how involved members of that community are in the decision making and practice of the organization, and what impact the organization ultimately has on the capacity of its community…are thus central factors in its effectiveness."[4] This interaction contributes to a healthier nonprofit sector and a more vigorous civil society, as shown in Figure 1: The Ripple Effect of Capacity Building, below.[5]

Figure 1: The Ripple Effect of Capacity Building

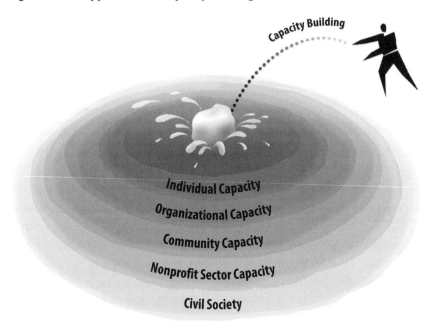

Think of capacity building as stone thrown into a pool. Its effects begin with the individual and then spread through the organization, the community it serves, the nonprofit sector as whole, and eventually all of civil society.

Groups of concerned citizens working together through neighborhood associations, community development corporations, schools, faith-based organizations, and business associations have tremendous impact addressing such needs as affordable housing, job training, quality education, business development, and new American resettlement. Nonprofits help make government at all levels accountable, create a rich cultural environment for our citizens, and advance scientific discoveries and medical research. All of these organizations are led by dedicated people committed to enriching and improving our lives. Strengthening these community leaders and these organizations builds the community's infrastructure and enhances life for all citizens. Capacity building at any level—individual, organizational, or community—will influence all other levels. Some funders deliberately focus on capacity building for the community and nonprofit sector levels. For example, the Charles Stewart Mott Foundation's national civil society grantmaking focuses primarily on building the infrastructure of the nonprofit sector. The Annie E. Casey Foundation provides technical assistance and tools to community-based organizations as part of its Rebuilding Communities Initiative.

Leverage philanthropic dollars

Investing in capacity building is an effective way to leverage—and ultimately multiply—the impact of philanthropic resources. Writing in the *Harvard Business Review*, Michael Porter and Mark Kramer explain: "By helping grantees to improve their own capabilities, foundations can affect the social productivity of more resources than just their slice of the whole." Porter and Kramer point out that "foundations can create still more value if they move beyond the role of capital provider to the role of fully engaged partner, thereby improving the grantee's effectiveness as an organization."[6] They argue that funders frequently create disincentives to good management by emphasizing new programs and focusing on the short term. They suggest that foundations can improve the performance of grant recipients by awarding grants for management development, enabling access to professional service firms, and providing advice directly.

As a funder, you can create still greater value by investing in expanding and sharing knowledge, which includes supporting the identification of best-practices, theoretical and applied research, and writing and publishing. Your unique vantage point can also help service delivery systems and communities identify and address trends and opportunities that are difficult to recognize or tackle by a single nonprofit. Investing in capacity building helps the entire funding community reach its goals, since by sharing the load of capacity building, all programs are strengthened. Additionally, funders benefit through enhanced partnership with grantees, positive community relations, better information on the impact of funding, and increased knowledge that can be applied to their own organizations.

Chapter Summary

This chapter defined capacity building as the process of strengthening an organization in order to improve its performance and impact. Capacity building is not new, but during the last five to ten years funders have shown increased interest in and support for improving organizational infrastructure. Grantmakers support capacity building for three primary reasons: to enhance program impact, increase nonprofit and community sustainability, and leverage philanthropic dollars.

The remainder of this book will explore in greater depth the strategic choices involved in providing capacity building support to nonprofits. Chapter 2: What Capacity Building Is will examine the components of capacity building and describe the most common capacity building approaches used by nonprofits.

Chapter 2

What Capacity Building Is

C HAPTER 1 COVERED REASONS TO INVEST IN CAPACITY BUILD-
ing. This chapter provides an overview of the field of capacity
building, including components of nonprofit organizational capacity, characteristics of high-performing groups, and various types of
capacity building activities, as well as ways that capacity builders can assist
nonprofits.

Capacity is an abstract term that describes a wide range of capabilities,
knowledge, and resources that nonprofits need in order to be effective.
What makes an organization effective? According to Grantmakers for Effective Organizations, it is "the ability of an organization to fulfill its mission
through a blend of sound management, strong governance, and a persistent
rededication to achieving results."[7] Organizational capacity is multifaceted
and continually evolving. Figure 2 depicts the elements of nonprofit organizational capacity.

The model shown in Figure 2 includes six components of organizational
capacity that are necessary for high performance: mission, vision, and
strategy; governance and leadership; program delivery and impact; strategic relationships; resource development; and internal operations and
management. These interdependent factors all contribute to the health and
performance of a nonprofit organization. The model also suggests continual
interaction between the organization's external environment and its internal components.[8]

Figure 2: Components of Organizational Capacity

Organizational capacity consists of six interdependent components, all of which interact with the external environment.

Mission, Vision, and Strategy: The organization has a vital mission and a clear understanding of its identity. It is able to clearly articulate organizational values. It is actively involved in regular, results-oriented, strategic, and self-reflective thinking and planning that aligns strategies with the mission, values, and organizational capacity. The planning process involves stakeholders in an ongoing dialogue that ensures that the organization's mission and programs are valuable to the constituency it serves.

Governance and Leadership: Members of the organization's board of directors are engaged and representative, with defined governance practices. The board effectively oversees the policies, programs, and organizational operations including review of achievement of strategic goals, financial status, and executive director performance. The organization is accomplished at recruiting, developing, and retaining capable staff and technical resources. The organization's leadership is alert to changing community needs and realities.

Program Delivery and Impact: The organization operates programs and conducts activities that demonstrate tangible outcomes and impact appropriate to the resources invested. Programs are high quality and well regarded. The organization utilizes program evaluation results to inform its strategic goals. The organization understands community needs and has formal mechanisms for assessing internal and external factors that affect the achievement of goals.

Strategic Relationships: The organization is a respected and active participant and leader in the community, and maintains strong connections with its constituents. It participates in strategic alliances and partnerships that significantly advance the organization's goals and expand its influence. It communicates well with external audiences.

Resource Development: The organization successfully secures support from a variety of sources to ensure its revenues are diversified, stable, and sufficient for the mission and goals. The resource development plan is aligned with the mission, long-term goals, and strategic direction. The organization has high visibility with key stakeholders and links clear, strategic messages to its resource development efforts.

Internal Operations and Management: The organization has efficient and effective operations and strong management support systems. Financial operations are responsibly managed and reflect sound accounting principles. The organization utilizes information effectively for organizational and project management purposes. Internal communications are effective, and the organization's culture promotes high-quality work and respectful work relationships. Asset, risk, and technology management is strong and appropriate to the organization's purpose.

Each of the components serves a critical role in an organization's overall effectiveness. Mission, vision, and strategy are the driving forces that give the organization its purpose and direction. Program delivery and impact are the nonprofit's primary reasons for existence, just as profit is a primary aim for most businesses. Strategic relationships, resource development, and internal operations and management are all necessary mechanisms to achieve the organization's ends. Governance and Leadership are the lubricant that keeps all the parts aligned and moving. All of these components are affected by the environment in which the organization exists.

When assessing nonprofits and planning intervention strategies, capacity builders need to examine each component separately, in relation to the others, and within the organization's overall context. Organizations operate as complex systems in which a change in any one part of the system affects other parts and the functioning of the whole. For example, a change in leadership will affect the organizational culture, which can in turn change productivity levels and financial performance, for the better or worse.

In addition, a variety of factors can influence an organization's needs at any time, including

- Age and developmental stage of the organization
- Size of the organization
- Kind of work the organization does
- Cultural or ethnic identity of the organization
- Environment in which the organization functions

These factors require capacity building activities that are uniquely tailored to the organization.

Capacity Building Activities

Capacity building refers to activities that strengthen a nonprofit organization and help it better fulfill its mission. These activities include, among others, strategic planning, technology upgrades, operational improvements, and board development. The sidebar shows the wide variety of types of capacity building activities. Capacity building can advance an organization's ability to deliver programs, expand, and be adaptive and innovative.[9]

Capacity Building Activities

Mission, Vision, and Strategy

- Strategic planning
- Scenario planning
- Organizational assessment
- Organizational development

Governance and Leadership

- Leadership development
- Board development
- Executive transition

Program Delivery and Impact

- Program design and development
- Evaluation

Strategic Relationships

- Collaboration and strategic restructuring
- Marketing and communications

Resource Development

- Fund development
- Business planning for revenue-generating activities

Internal Operations and Management

- Human resource management and training
- Financial management
- Operations
- Technology and information systems
- Facility planning
- Legal issues
- Volunteer recruitment and management
- Conflict resolution

19

Means of Providing Assistance

Nonprofit managers and trustees usually work on their own to improve organizational performance by planning on an ongoing basis; providing stronger management and oversight; hiring new staff; training staff; upgrading systems; acquiring new equipment; and renovating and purchasing facilities. Indeed, much organizational development work is a sensitive inside job that the organizations themselves *must* do on their own. Often, however, nonprofits turn to outside individuals and groups—capacity building providers—to support their capacity building needs. These providers include researchers, writers, publishers, trainers, educators, facilitators, and consultants. (See the sidebar Capacity Building Providers on page 23 for more details.) They assist nonprofits through referrals, research, publishing, education and training, peer exchanges, and consulting, as described in detail below.

Referrals

One way to help nonprofits is to direct them to resources that can help them address organizational challenges and opportunities. Grantmakers and management assistance providers can refer nonprofits to useful web sites, written materials, workshops, courses, and consultants, as well as to other nonprofits that have faced similar challenges.

Research

Research related to nonprofit management and governance can help develop models and tools for nonprofit leaders to use. Researchers can also assess the effectiveness of the organization's performance and of various capacity building activities.

Publications

There are many publications—in print and increasingly online—related to nonprofit management and governance. They include practical, hands-on, how-to guides and journals filled with checklists and sample forms, as well as academic articles and books that report on research and explain theories and concepts. Nonprofit staff and board members can apply knowledge gleaned from these materials to their own situation to enhance the effectiveness of their organization.

Education and training

Organizational capacity building efforts address the needs of the individuals who staff an organization. Training and educational opportunities enable employees, trustees, and volunteers to develop skills to help them do a better job managing, overseeing, and supporting their organization. Offerings can range from brief, one-shot seminars to yearlong, university-based courses. While some seminars are led by an instructor who imparts knowledge within a set curriculum, others are coordinated by a facilitator who helps people within an organization or from different organizations share with and learn from each other. Increasingly, distance-learning opportunities are being offered online. Whatever the format, adults learn best when there is a clear agenda with specific goals and when there is an opportunity to apply new skills and concepts to real-life work situations.

Peer exchanges

Peer exchanges—including roundtables, case-study groups, and learning circles—are based on the premise that participants can be both teachers and learners. To be most successful, peer exchanges need a skilled facilitator, a safe environment in which participants can express and modify their beliefs, and a balance of structure and flexibility. Peer exchanges can lessen the isolation of participants, help them become more self-confident, and heighten their awareness of diverse views and alternate solutions.

Convening

The term *convening* refers to bringing together various nonprofits or leaders in one setting. Nonprofits have considerably more power to influence funding trends, complex community issues, or developmental challenges when they band together. Convening can facilitate joint action. Meetings allow nonprofit leaders to learn from each other, collectively set agendas, and organize joint efforts. Conferences and forums can enable nonprofit executives to plan ways to increase the effectiveness of their organization and field and enhance their community, as well as advocate for policies that can increase their nonprofit's efficiency and impact.

Consulting

Consulting is a broad term that describes a wide array of relationships between a nonprofit client and a professional advisor, whether an independent consultant, nonprofit management support organization, or private consulting firm. Consulting roles vary depending on the consultant's style and background, the needs of the client, and the type of project. In some cases, a consultant acts primarily as a directive expert, conveying information and prescribing solutions related to programs, organizational development, or specialized areas such as accounting or fundraising. In other situations, a consultant plays the role of a facilitator, guiding a process and collaboratively helping the client to reflect on options and make decisions. More consultants are serving as coaches to nonprofit executives by offering new ideas and perspectives, asking challenging questions, and helping to process information and adapt behavior. Consulting engagements are most successful when the advisor and client agree on goals and strategies, have clear mutual expectations, share a commitment to making change, and dedicate adequate time to the effort.

A note on providing assistance

Outside capacity building resources offer objectivity and expertise to help the nonprofit examine its performance and develop appropriate ways to improve effectiveness. But frequently, what nonprofits need most to support this capacity building work is *money*. See Chapter 4: Capacity Building Strategies for various approaches funders can take to provide financial support for this work.

Capacity Building Providers

There is great variety in the focus, depth, and breadth of capacity building resources available in different communities. More resources tend to be available in urban areas than in rural areas. And North America and Europe tend to have more providers than other continents. In North America, many of these capacity builders belong to the Alliance for Nonprofit Management, a professional association with over six hundred members, dedicated to "increasing the effectiveness of individuals and organizations that help nonprofits build their power and impact."

The following list describes different types of capacity building providers.

Management support organizations (MSOs)—nonprofit consulting and training groups, sometimes volunteer-based and sometimes professionally staffed. Examples include CompassPoint Nonprofit Services in San Francisco, the Center for Nonprofit Management in Dallas, LaSalle University's Nonprofit Management and Development Center in Philadelphia, or the International Council on Management of Population Programmes in Malaysia. Some MSOs have a local or regional focus; some are national or international in scope. They may also differ in their organizational concentration (planning, board development, marketing), industry focus (arts, education, immigrant organizations), staffing model (volunteers, affiliated independent contractors, or paid staff providers), fee basis (from totally subsidized to market rate), and level of experience and quality.

Intermediary organizations—nonprofits that provide an array of support including capacity building assistance, re-granting, loan and equity programs, research, convening, and advocacy. Often funders use intermediaries to help them build capacity with networks of nonprofits, rather than dealing individually with each nonprofit. For example, Amherst H. Wilder Foundation's Center for Communities offers a full range of research, consulting, training, and publishing services, community grant initiatives, and community development support to the local community. Local Initiatives Support Corporation (LISC) provides grants, loans, equity investments, and other capacity building assistance to community development corporations. The Hispanic Federation offers fund development, grantmaking, technical assistance services, and advocacy.

Community support organizations (CSOs)—intermediary organizations dedicated to improving the way the community solves problems[10] such as the Collaboratory for Community Support in Ann Arbor, Michigan, or the Community Development Institute in Oakland, California. CSOs provide capacity building support to communities in much the same way that MSOs support nonprofit organizations.

Research groups—groups specializing in evaluation or offering full-service research. Chapin Hall Center for Children or the Urban Institute are examples. Many research groups are affiliated with universities and colleges.

Academic institutions—business schools and programs in nonprofit management, public policy, communications, and organizational development such as the Hauser Center for Nonprofit Organizations at Harvard University.

Independent consultants—numerous individuals with varying levels of experience and skill working with nonprofits. No certification or licensing body regulates who can hang a shingle as a consultant or trainer.

For-profit consulting firms—firms specializing in nonprofit and philanthropic issues, such as the Conservation Company, as well as large corporate strategy firms that have nonprofit practices, such as McKinsey & Company.

Retired executives—individuals who provide services independently or through professional associations or organized community service programs such as Service Corps of Retired/Active Executives (SCORE) or the Small Business Association.

State associations of nonprofits—organizations that provide advocacy, support, information, and networking for nonprofits such as the Minnesota Council on Nonprofits or the Maryland Association of Nonprofit Organizations.

Chapter Summary

Capacity building refers to activities that enhance the effectiveness of a nonprofit organization, such as leadership development, business planning, and improvements in financial management systems. Mission, vision, and strategy; governance and leadership; program delivery and impact; strategic relationships; resource development; and internal operations and management all contribute to organizational capacity. While nonprofit leaders frequently improve the performance of their organization on their own, they are sometimes assisted by capacity builders through referrals, research, publications, education and training, peer exchanges, convening, and consulting.

Chapter 3: How to Build the Capacity of Nonprofits describes a flexible four-step process that funders can follow to plan, implement, and evaluate a capacity building effort with nonprofits. Chapter 4: Capacity Building Strategies examines approaches funders can use to enhance the organizational effectiveness of nonprofits.

Chapter 3

How to Build the Capacity of Nonprofits

THE PREVIOUS CHAPTERS EXPLAINED WHAT CAPACITY BUILDING is and why to invest in it. This chapter has two parts: the first part includes lessons learned from funders that have been involved in capacity building work. The second part describes a four-step process that you can follow to plan, implement, and evaluate a capacity building effort.

Lessons Learned

The work of building effective nonprofit organizations is difficult, complex, demanding—and rewarding. There is no single right way to do capacity building. But there are some general lessons learned from the experience of funders that may make your efforts more effective.

- Follow other funders' promising practices
- Do no harm
- Develop clear expectations regarding confidentiality and communication
- Build on nonprofits' strengths
- Remember that one size does not fit all
- Be patient and flexible

- Coordinate efforts with other funders
- Hold your own organization to the same standards you expect of others
- Keep the focus on mission

As your work proceeds, learn from your experience and make midcourse corrections. (See the sidebar Learning from Your Mistakes on page 27. For lessons learned from international funders, see Appendix A.)

Follow other funders' promising practices

Before embarking on a new capacity building initiative, learn what other funders are doing and what they've learned and consult the relevant research. Why reinvent the wheel or pursue a strategy that has proven to be ineffective? The sidebar Key Success Factors for Effective Capacity Building identifies good practices in supporting capacity building. Organizations such as Grantmakers for Effective Organizations and the Alliance for Non-

Key Success Factors for Effective Capacity Building

The Human Interaction Research Institute recently conducted a study of funders' capacity building efforts. This study, *Strengthening Nonprofits: Capacity Building and Philanthropy*, found that the most effective capacity building activities initiated or operated by foundations demonstrate the following characteristics.

Readiness-based—they occur when the client is ready to receive this specialized kind of service.

Timely—they are done neither too slowly to be relevant nor too quickly to allow the work to produce results in a complex context.

Assessment-based—they begin with a thorough assessment of the needs and assets of the organization and the community in which it operates, which in turn drives the types of capacity building services provided.

Customized—they are tailored to the type of organization or group, its culture and community environment, and its developmental stage.

Contextualized—they occur within the context of other capacity building an organization is receiving and relevant forces in its environment.

Peer-connected—they happen when there are opportunities for peer-to-peer networking, mentoring, and information sharing.

Competence-based—they are offered by reputable providers and requested by nonprofits that are knowledgeable and sophisticated customers.

Comprehensive—while narrowly defined approaches can work, the highest impact activities are part of one-stop shopping in which customers can access a full range of capacity building services.[11]

profit Management are helping to establish clearinghouses for ideas related to organizational effectiveness. Take advantage of these resources and adapt what others have done for your own work. (See Appendix B: Resources on page 118.)

Learning from Your Mistakes

You are bound, at some point, to engage in capacity building efforts that don't get the desired results. The following are examples from three funders who learned from experience and made improvements.

- The Eugene and Agnes E. Meyer Foundation's original attempts to provide technology support for its grantees did not work out well. As Mary Ann Holohean of the Meyer Foundation observes, "Not only was our support not helpful in strengthening the grantee's use of technology, but it was contributing to the organization's further discouragement about its ability to use technology effectively." The foundation realized that grantees were not informed consumers of technology services and lacked access to front-end help analyzing their needs. Therefore, the foundation changed its strategy to support technology consultants who first helped the nonprofits assess their technology needs, and it created a regional technology solutions network—Technology Works for Good—to support effective use of technology. This strategy has enabled the nonprofit organizations to understand their needs better and be more informed consumers of technological services.

- The Mary Reynolds Babcock Foundation had to make some midcourse corrections with its organizational development program for small, grassroots groups. The foundation originally made three-year grant commitments (with two grants of eighteen months each) to a set of organizations for core operating support and specific capacity building work. When the grantees first reported on their progress, the foundation learned that few were doing any significant organizational

development work at all, although the foundation had negotiated specific capacity building goals and connected several of the groups with consultants. Gayle Williams of the Babcock Foundation notes, "We realized that our grants could do harm by giving [grantees] an infusion of money for three years without building their capacity to sustain higher budgets and bigger programmatic work plans." Beyond program delivery, grantees had little energy left over for organizational development, did not really know how to build an organization, and did not know where to get the help they needed. As a result, the foundation regrouped and decided to fund fewer organizations each year and put more money into organizational assessments, technical assistance, and grassroots fundraising training.

- In 1995, the Ford Foundation launched the Working Capital Fund, which provides working capital and consulting assistance to midsize arts groups. The goal is to build durable and sustainable organizations. In its first round of grants, some of the participants ran into difficulties. Writing about the program, Susan Kenny Stevens and Diane Espaldon state, "As program designers and operators, we learned the hard way that participant readiness is the foundation for a successful capacity program." They note that several groups were not ready to take full advantage of the program. One organization was not able to devote enough time to the program and another did not have the adequate will to change. In the next round, the foundation screened groups more carefully to determine their readiness to participate in and benefit from the program.[12]

Do no harm

Funders wield tremendous power in their communities. Even with the best of intentions to collaborate with nonprofit groups, truly equal alliances are rare. A casual comment by a funder can easily be misinterpreted as a judgment, suggestion, or warning by a grant seeker or grantee. When a funder engages in capacity building—a process that often matches an "expert" with an organization somehow viewed as lacking knowledge or resources—the power disparity widens. Your challenge is to use your power wisely and do no harm. Support the capacity building of nonprofits in ways that strengthen and restore them, rather than emasculate them.

Although making capacity building a condition of funding can be a powerful strategy, it can also be viewed as manipulative and interfering by potential grantees. Rather than requiring capacity building, you might want to just state clearly the programmatic or organizational outcomes you expect, and leave it up to the grantee to figure out how to achieve them, offering help if the grantee requests it. Successful capacity building depends on the will of the organization to strengthen itself; it cannot be imposed from the outside.

Build trusting relationships with nonprofits. Keep in mind that many nonprofits are inexperienced at organizational development and unaccustomed to having funders interested in how their organization is functioning. Try to share your perspective and experience with nonprofit organizations without creating obligations or exerting undue influence. If grant recipients ask for suggestions about possible resources, share your ideas carefully. If you do not have a close, trusting relationship with a nonprofit, be cautious about giving management advice, and avoid being overly intrusive. A meddlesome grantmaker can sometimes worsen an organization's situation. Some capacity builders or nonprofits, fearing a possible loss of funding, may follow a grantmaker's unwise advice, with damaging results.

Develop clear expectations regarding confidentiality and communication

Funders, capacity builders, and nonprofit organizations frequently become engaged in a triangular relationship.[13] This occurs when a funder supports a nonprofit in purchasing the services of a management assistance provider, funds a capacity builder to assist nonprofits, or has a capacity builder on retainer to provide services. (The dynamics of the relationship are different when a funder provides management assistance directly to a nonprofit or has a capacity builder on retainer to provide such services.)

Figure 3: A Delicate Balance

The Relationship of Funder, Capacity Builder, and Nonprofit

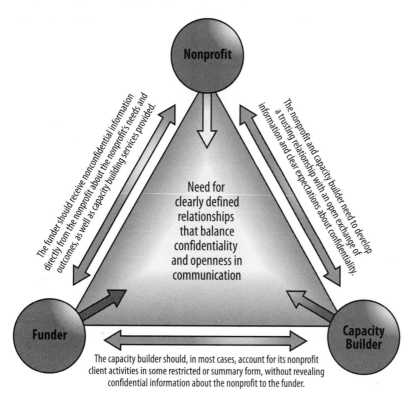

Need for clearly defined relationships that balance confidentiality and openness in communication

The funder should receive nonconfidential information directly from the nonprofit about the nonprofit's needs and outcomes, as well as capacity building services provided.

The nonprofit and capacity builder need to develop a trusting relationship with an open exchange of information and clear expectations about confidentiality.

The capacity builder should, in most cases, account for its nonprofit client activities in some restricted or summary form, without revealing confidential information about the nonprofit to the funder.

As depicted in Figure 3: A Delicate Balance, the funder must strike the right balance of confidentiality and openness appropriate to each of the three sides in this partnership, respecting boundaries while encouraging communication. Information is power, and it must be distributed judiciously to keep this delicate relationship functioning well. The nonprofit and capacity builder need to trust each other, exchange information freely, and establish clear expectations about confidentiality. To improve its management and governance, a nonprofit often must "air its dirty laundry" to assistance providers. This leaves the nonprofit exposed. The capacity builder must respect this vulnerability in accounting to the funder. In most cases, client activities can be reported in a restricted or summary form, providing relevant material about organizational needs, capacity building services, and outcomes without revealing privileged information. Three-way meetings at the start and end of a capacity building project can clarify expectations and minimize perceptions of collusion.

The extent to which the funder is privy to all the details of the nonprofit's development experience is an important decision to resolve at the beginning of a capacity building process. In the short term, there is comfort for a funder in knowing what the issues are and what the plan is for addressing them within a nonprofit. In the long term, the nonprofit itself has to grapple with its own development challenges, and learn to ask for help when necessary and from whomever is best qualified to give it. If your participation in the details of the capacity building experience is a requirement of your funding, it is best to be up front about that requirement, and negotiate how communications will occur from the beginning.

If you provide management assistance directly to a nonprofit and also act as the grantmaker, you can be at two points in the triangulated relationship. In this case, invest time to build trusting relationships with program grantees and be as transparent as possible with them. You might consider explicitly stating to grant recipients that they will not be penalized for revealing management problems and that program funding will only be jeopardized if they fail to achieve program outcomes.

Build on nonprofits' strengths

Capacity building work for nonprofit organizations should concentrate on building on assets, not on correcting weaknesses. In fact, the act of initiating capacity building is a sign of strength and effectiveness within an organization; it recognizes that every organization needs improvement and adaptation to changing circumstances from time to time. Do not treat nonprofits as sick patients that need treatment for their ailments and funders and capacity builders as doctors. Instead, meet nonprofits where they are and capitalize on what works well. Jan Masaoka, executive director of CompassPoint Nonprofit Services, observes that if capacity builders begin to think of nonprofits "as Olympic-potential athletes, and ourselves as their coaches, [we] might start by helping an organization build on its strengths—whether that's strong executive leadership, a strong board, or great community support."[14]

Remember that one size does not fit all

Make sure that management assistance is tailored to organizational need. Encourage applicants or grantees to reflect on what their capacity building needs are, and what style and kind of assistance might be most helpful to them. Nonprofits at different stages of organizational development need different types of help. Although some nonprofits can benefit from strategic planning, others may not need or be ready for it. Context also matters: When an organization is in crisis, for example, an outside consultant trying to conduct a visioning exercise may be the last thing it needs. Nonprofit leaders also have varied learning styles. Some learn best by reading or listening to an expert lecture, but others benefit most from one-on-one coaching and peer mentoring.

Be patient and flexible

Organizational capacity building is a time-consuming and complex process. Avoid creating inflated expectations for guaranteed, positive results over a short period. To succeed, you must be flexible, patient, and willing to take risks. After managing a program that provided management assistance to youth-serving organizations, the Fund for the City of New York advised nonprofit executives that "hiring a consultant means that the leaders and managers will have more, not less, work to do."[15] Make sure everyone involved in your capacity building effort understands that change takes hard work. As the evaluator of the James Irvine Foundation's project to enhance the effectiveness of employment and training organizations points out, "The importance of investing time in conveying the project's value and being explicit about the work involved should not be underestimated."[16]

Similarly, building organizational capacity is not a short-term proposition. Based on its ten years of experience providing capacity building assistance to nonprofits, the Milton S. Eisenhower Foundation concluded that it usually takes at least thirty-six months for measurable positive outcomes to occur. [17] Some funders believe that a five- to ten-year investment is needed to make a difference.

Coordinate efforts with other funders

Consider collaborating with other funders on your effort. By strategically selecting partners, you can offer a greater range of expertise and more resources. For example, the Eugene and Agnes E. Meyer Foundation is partnering with the Fannie Mae Foundation and Community Wealth Ventures to build the capacity of nonprofits in the Washington, D.C., area to capitalize on their assets, and build business ventures, strategic alliances, and new revenue streams. You and other grantmakers might pool funds designated for capacity building purposes. Another possibility is to coordinate your work with government agencies, many of which support management assistance for their nonprofit contractors and grantees. Collaboration allows you and other funders to build on each other's strengths, learn from each other, avoid duplicating staff capabilities, and give your grantees one consistent message.

Hold your own organization to the same standards you expect of others

You can't expect grantees to measure up to standards your own organization is not meeting. The discrepancy between principles and practice is keenly observed by grant recipients who may resent being held to a standard higher than that to which the funder holds itself. Funders should "walk their talk."

You can go through a systematic assessment of your own organization later in this chapter, in Step 2: Take Stock.

Keep the focus on mission

Effective management and governance are means for nonprofit organizations to achieve their mission and vision; they are not ends in themselves. The ends are the specific long-term impacts you want to achieve at the organizational, programmatic, and community level. An excessive focus on professionalism and business models can bury idealism or distract from an organization's purpose. As William Ryan, a fellow at Harvard's Hauser Center for Nonprofit Organizations, cautions, "There is a growing discomfort by many within the sector that a corporate ideology of 'managerialism' is threatening to displace the values and passion that nonprofits aspire to."[18]

The Four-Step Process

The decision to begin or expand a capacity building funding effort requires careful planning and research. Many decisions made during planning can have major implications for your organization. The following pages describe a four-step process you can use to plan and carry out your capacity building work.

> **Step 1: Plan to Plan** helps you create a planning process that will result in a solid plan. It also helps you line up needed resources.

Step 2: Take Stock includes assessing your own organization's readiness and capabilities for starting a capacity building effort, reviewing needs and opportunities in the community, and identifying your organization's values.

Step 3: Set Direction involves establishing goals and objectives, selecting capacity building strategies, and committing resources.

Step 4: Take Action and Evaluate covers implementation and evaluation approaches and tools.

You can follow the process from start to finish, or you can go to the specific step that you may be working on. This chapter describes specific tasks for each step and particular actions for each task. Appendix C provides worksheets for each step. Use them to document your decisions and plans.

The four steps are laid out as a linear and sequential process. In practice, the process is dynamic and iterative. You may need to work some steps simultaneously or go back to a previous step to gather additional information before moving forward. The process is also ongoing and cyclical, since, after implementing and evaluating the effectiveness of your strategies, you will begin a new round of planning, goal setting, and strategy development. Figure 4: Four Steps to Support Capacity Building provides an overview of the process.

Figure 4: Four Steps to Support Capacity Building

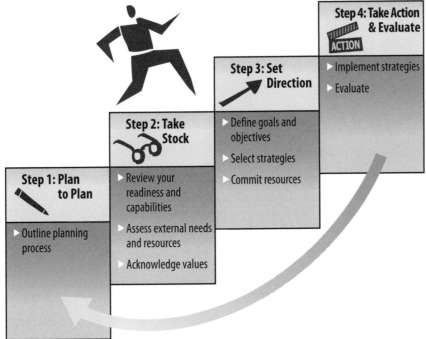

Step 1: Plan to Plan
- Outline planning process

Step 2: Take Stock
- Review your readiness and capabilities
- Assess external needs and resources
- Acknowledge values

Step 3: Set Direction
- Define goals and objectives
- Select strategies
- Commit resources

Step 4: Take Action & Evaluate
ACTION
- Implement strategies
- Evaluate

Shortcuts

The planning process delineated in this chapter is comprehensive, detailed, and deliberate. If you find it to be too resource-intensive, overwhelming, or rigid, simplify the process to fit your needs. See the "shortcut" sidebars at the beginning of each of the four steps for tips on how to streamline the step.

Step 1: Plan to Plan

Building capacity is building for the future. The work must be sound, beginning with the foundation. Your capacity building plan needs to fit with your organization's mission and values, take into account both internal resources and external needs and opportunities, and incorporate strategies that will achieve the desired impact.

You can plan your capacity building efforts, at least in the beginning, as a separate initiative, or you might want to integrate your planning for capacity building into your organization's comprehensive strategic planning process. Design a systematic planning process that takes into account your

Shortcut for Step 1

Step 1: Plan to Plan can be very straightforward if you decide not to use outside consulting assistance and want to involve only one or two board or staff members. Simply outline a planning process and schedule that will work for your organization.

experience, the commitment of your organization's leaders, and the amount of time and resources available for planning. Four tasks need attention in designing a planning process.

Task One: Establish a general approach and pace for your planning process

Task Two: Determine who will be involved with the planning process

Task Three: Decide whether you need outside help

Task Four: Create a timeline for your planning process

Use Worksheet 1: Design Your Planning Process in Appendix C (page 130) to record decisions about your planning process.

Task One: Establish a general approach and pace for your planning process

The four-step process described in this chapter is flexible and can be modified for your circumstances. Tailor a process that will work for your organization. If you are starting from scratch, you may want to go through Steps 1 through 3 deliberatively and invest a lot of time in each one. If you are already implementing capacity building strategies, you may choose to go through all the steps quickly to determine how to improve or supplement your existing strategies. Or, you could skip some of Steps 1 through 3 and just focus on Step 4, where you evaluate your current strategy.

A typical planning process will take three to six months, but it can take less or more time depending on your particular situation. The duration depends on the scope of the planned initiative, the level of trust and agreement among planning group members, and the degree of stakeholder involvement in the process.

Task Two: Determine who will be involved with the planning process

Before formally taking the steps described in this chapter, identify the individuals you believe are best suited to participate in planning your capacity building efforts. Form a planning committee comprising a core group of people who are deeply committed to and engaged with the work, such as the executive director of your organization and key board and staff members. This group is the hub for consultation, negotiation, and problem solving throughout the entire process. Try to identify one committee member who will lead and champion the process.

Certain steps will require the input of specific individuals who may not be appropriate for inclusion in the planning committee, such as specialized employees, board committee members, and "outsiders" including representatives from management assistance providers and other nonprofit organizations. For example, the Irene E. and George A. Davis Foundation, based in Springfield, Massachusetts, formed an organizational effectiveness task force comprising representatives from local agencies and funders to help guide its effort.[19] Periodically, you might want to invite a larger group of board and staff members who are not on the planning committee to share their experiences and to help shape a vision for your organization's capacity building work. Broad participation will help to ensure that your chosen strategies are supported at all levels of your organization.

Task Three: Decide whether you need outside help

Early on, the planning committee should determine whether outside consulting assistance might be needed. A consultant can guide the entire process, facilitate a major meeting, learn about other funders' practices, or conduct organizational assessments. Consultants are especially valuable when you need additional expertise, a devil's advocate in the group, or even an extra set of hands. Other resources to consider include peer grantmakers, training sessions organized by regional grantmaker associations or affinity groups, and publications (see Appendix B).

Task Four: Create a timeline for your planning process

Make sure that you identify major tasks and key decision points during the planning process. Figure out how long you want to spend on each step. Be sure that you specify who is involved at each step and how much time is expected of the person. Identify the resources needed at the various stages. Worksheet 1 in Appendix C will help you lay out your planning process and schedule. As you proceed through the four steps, revisit, update, and revise your plan and add more detail.

Once you have outlined your planning process, you are ready for Step 2, in which you take stock of internal and external conditions.

Shortcut for Step 2

Step 2 can be accomplished fairly quickly, especially if you want to begin small and gradually scale up your capacity building efforts. Some hints for streamlining the review process:

- Be sure to pay attention to all three areas: internal strengths and liabilities; external needs and resources; and values and operating assumptions.

- Ask, What do we know now, and what information is most critical for us to understand before making decisions?

- Take advantage of research that has already been done on community or nonprofit needs.

- Tap the knowledge and experience of a few key informants in the community who have a broad view of the field.

- Enlist the help of a consultant or researcher who can quickly gather needed information and help you analyze it.

Step 2: Take Stock

Good plans are usually based on a solid understanding of the current situation, as well as an understanding of future needs and opportunities. Developing a plan to strengthen the effectiveness of nonprofits in your community requires the same level of study and rigor that any other planning process does.

Step 2: Take Stock entails three main tasks:

Task One: Determine your organization's readiness and capabilities

Task Two: Review external needs and resources

Task Three: Acknowledge your organization's values and assumptions

Your aim is to find the overlap among these three areas and choose strategies that reflect this fit. You can look at these three areas in whatever sequence makes sense to you, or you can work on them simultaneously. Worksheets 2A through 2C in Appendix C will guide you through these tasks.

Task One: Determine your organization's readiness and capabilities

As you consider launching a capacity building effort, or even shoring up an existing one, examine six aspects of your own organization: commitment, leadership, practices, financial resources, organizational assets, and reputation. There are two compelling reasons to do this. First, you will want to make sure that you have sufficient commitment, leadership, staff, and credibility in the community to engage with nonprofits in a new way. Second, you may need to build the capacity of your own organization—to ensure that you have sufficient strength to undertake this effort, and to ensure that you can speak with integrity about organizational effectiveness.

1. **Commitment:** There should be sufficient support throughout your organization to launch a capacity building effort and to commit to it long-term, perhaps five to ten years. Your biggest challenge may be convincing other staff, trustees, and donors that helping nonprofits build a strong base to ensure their continued programmatic success is as important as helping them address the needs of their constituents today. In fact, it may be more important. If commitment to capacity building is not part of your organization's mission, your stakeholders may need additional information about the potential benefits of strengthening nonprofit organizations. Or they may need to understand more fully what trends and challenges are affecting nonprofits in the community.

2. **Leadership:** Two aspects of leadership need to be considered: leadership of the planning effort, and future leadership of any capacity building efforts that you might undertake. Make sure the leader understands capacity building and is well-regarded within the organization and community.

3. **Practices:** Consider whether you pay adequate attention to your organization's own effectiveness. The discrepancy between standards and practice is keenly observed by grantees. If you expect nonprofits to invest in their own effectiveness, you need to model the same quest for learning and improvement that you expect of them. You also need

to understand enough about capacity building processes so that you understand what your grantees will be experiencing. Try answering the following questions to determine how well your funding organization practices what it preaches.

- How do our current grantmaking practices encourage or discourage grantees to build strong organizations?

- Is our mission clear, understood, and aligned with our current program efforts? Is it broad enough to include a focus on capacity building?

- Do we have an up-to-date strategic plan that is used, monitored, and updated?

- Do we regularly seek and use input from our constituencies in making programming decisions?

- Is our board clear about its roles and responsibilities? Is the governance structure effective?

- Are the board and staff representative of the diversity of the community we serve?

- Do we routinely collaborate with other organizations with similar missions, service areas, or funding priorities?

- Do we systematically evaluate the impact of our grantmaking and use that information to improve our funding practices?

4. **Financial Resources:** Assess whether your organization is prepared to commit resources to capacity building efforts for the long term. This may mean shifting funds away from other programmatic efforts. These decisions about financial allocations are directly related to your mission and organizational values and as such may require considerable deliberation. You won't know what specific level of resources you will need to support capacity building work until later in your planning process. But a general sense of the level of commitment your organization might be willing to make will help you weigh the feasibility of different strategies as you proceed with your planning.

5. **Organizational Assets:** Your organization probably possesses significant nonmonetary assets that can be of benefit to the community or the nonprofits it serves. These assets may be in the form of staff, trustee, or volunteer expertise; research capabilities; or knowledge of community resources. You may have financial or evaluation expertise, or a reputation as a neutral convener or facilitator. You might have meeting or conference space to offer. Take stock of the resources you bring to the table that might influence the strategies you select. Consider asking your grantees what assets they would value from your organizational "treasure chest." For example, the GE Fund has tapped General Electric employees to provide marketing and business planning assistance to nonprofits.[20]

   If you decide to proceed with capacity building activities, you need skilled staff who understand organizational capacity building and have the support of your organization to lead the effort. If you are thinking about providing direct management assistance to nonprofits through your own staff, you need specialized skills and knowledge in organizational assessment and intervention.

6. **Reputation:** Your organization will need the respect and trust of the community to undertake a capacity building venture. Assess whether nonprofits in the community regard you as a leader and trusted partner, and whether they are likely to be forthright about their challenges and needs. If the answer is no, or even maybe, you may need to strengthen your relationships before you proceed.

   The Mary Reynolds Babcock Foundation found that, even though it was viewed as a trusted supporter for program grants, it had to convince nonprofits that it really was interested in long-term effectiveness. Gayle Williams, the foundation's executive director, notes that "it takes at least a year before most nonprofits new to Babcock funding are trusting enough for us to begin having honest discussions about organizational health." The David and Lucile Packard Foundation periodically surveys its grantees to gain an understanding of their overall capacity building challenges and to obtain feedback on what grantees think of their support, according to Ruth Norris, senior program officer with Packard.

Discuss these six aspects of your organization's functioning with key people in your organization—either on a one-to-one basis or in groups. As you proceed with your review, use Worksheet 2A: Determine Your Organization's Readiness and Capabilities on page 132 to record the information you collect.

After reviewing the six aspects of your organization—commitment, leadership, practices, financial resources, organizational assets, and reputation—you will know whether your organization is poised to engage in funding capacity building approaches. You may have identified some interesting opportunities for leveraging your assets—financial or nonmonetary. You also will understand your organization's level of commitment to capacity building, and what aspects of your organization may need to be strengthened as you proceed. The Edna McConnell Clark Foundation, when launching its capacity building efforts, found that it first needed to work on its own organization. It had to change the skill set of staff, clarify its theory of change, develop ways to exit old programs, and build board commitment to longer-term change efforts.

You may discover some things that cause you to question the wisdom of proceeding with planning. These potential "showstoppers" might include

- Mission-based or bylaw restrictions related to providing capacity building support
- Severe lack of interest or commitment from leadership—either trustees or staff
- Current or pending change in organizational leadership
- Reluctance to make a long-term commitment to capacity building

If these or similar obstacles are present, your organization should address the obstacles before proceeding with capacity building efforts.

When you finish your internal review—and if you've found no insurmountable showstoppers—you can begin looking *outside* your organization at the needs and resources existing in your community. The next task, Review External Needs and Resources, will walk you through the external review.

Task Two: Review external needs and resources

Whether you want to revamp or expand your capacity building work, or whether you're entering a capacity building effort for the first time, a thorough assessment of community and nonprofit needs and resources will ground your decisions and enhance your chance for success.

This task involves two main actions:

1. Assess nonprofit and community needs
2. Assess community resources

The sidebar Methods for Assessing External Needs and Resources on page 48 offers techniques to help you work on this task. Be aware, however, that much of the information you're looking for may already be available. Before you invest a lot of time and money, check out whether any other grantmaker or nonprofit association has conducted surveys or studies asking questions similar to yours.

The external assessment helps you determine supply and demand issues related to capacity building—that is, who needs what, and who is available to provide it. Understanding both supply and demand will help you craft a capacity building strategy that achieves the desired impact. You can use Worksheet 2B: Review External Needs and Resources on page 135 to record your findings.

Assess nonprofit and community needs

Before you begin the needs assessment, decide whom you will ask about the capacity building needs of the community, how you will collect data, who will conduct the data collection, and what your timeline will be for completing the data collection. It is important to have a skilled person with experience and sensitivity conduct the needs assessment; otherwise you risk focusing on symptoms or on an area that will not get the results you hope for.

Consider the following questions about the needs of the organizations or community that you hope to impact.

1. **Whom will you target?**

   Before you begin to explore what assets and needs exist with nonprofits or in the broader community, you will have to define your target audience. You might look at current grant recipients or extend your inquiry to all nonprofits in a specific geographic area. You could focus on organizations working in a particular field, such as education or the environment, or on all entities—citizens, informal groups, nonprofits, public and private organizations—working to improve the community.

2. **What are your audience's strengths?**

   Inquire about the strengths of the nonprofits or community you are targeting. There may be outstanding nonprofits that serve as models of a resilient organization. There may be some exceptional executive directors or boards who have strong track records and are held in high regard. Or there may be networks that are effectively connecting and assisting nonprofits. Nonprofits in your target group may be especially good at outreach or forming alliances to achieve efficiencies in their operations. Any of these assets could be built on as part of your capacity building strategy.

3. **What trends are affecting your target audience?**

   Ask whether specific trends—such as in demographics, public policy, the economy, or technology—are creating new challenges for the community as you define it. (See the sidebar on page 10, A Sampling of Trends Affecting Nonprofits.)

4. **What does your target audience need?**

   Find out what capacity building activities are needed by nonprofits or in your community. (See the sidebar Capacity Building Activities on page 19 and the Means of Providing Assistance section on page 20 for ideas.) If you are interested in influencing broader community challenges, a particular field, or the nonprofit sector in a certain country, see the sidebar Some Areas Where Communities May Need to Improve for ideas. As you determine needs, look for patterns in needs or clusters of organizations that have similar needs.

When assessing capacity building needs, keep in mind three points: 1) nonprofits and communities are complex systems 2) their needs vary; and 3) the assessment you are conducting is itself a form of intervention.

1. **Nonprofit organizations and communities are complex systems.** Difficulty in one area may be a clue to other issues that need to be addressed. For instance, an executive director may believe that her organization needs the most help with fundraising; however, the organization's lack of fundraising success may actually be due to unclear goals, weak leadership, or board apathy. Board development and strategic planning may be more effective interventions. Changes in one area may impact other areas. For example, strengthening community-organizing skills in a neighborhood association may lead to heightened conflicts between the neighborhood and the city.

2. **Needs vary depending on the organization or community's stage of development.** Boards in start-up organizations and mature institutions need to function differently and require different kinds of development opportunities. Community planning in a stable neighborhood may look very different from community planning in a highly transitional neighborhood. Community planning for an arts

Some Areas Where Communities May Need to Improve

- Building community-wide consensus on critical issues—for example, affordable housing
- Citizen participation
- Collaboration between organizations or sectors
- Community studies and trend analysis
- Community visioning and planning
- Convening citizens, community leaders, and policy makers
- Determining the assets and needs of the community
- Leadership development
- Public education
- Racial tensions
- Resource development
- Service delivery systems
- Technology and communication systems
- Volunteer recruitment

district will be very different from a planning process for improved schools.

3. **Assessment in and of itself is a powerful intervention.** When you ask nonprofits about their needs, they may start thinking in new ways about their own effectiveness. You may also create expectations that you will be doing something—solving problems or providing funding. And as you talk to people, you will be consciously or inadvertently expressing your own values and beliefs about capacity building, and you will be forging relationships in the community. Proceed with caution, and with a sense of inquiry, honesty, and partnership.

Assess community resources

Examining existing community resources is the supply side of external assessment. In this action, you learn who is already providing capacity building support to nonprofits in the community, how accessible they are to nonprofits, and how effective they are. You determine if some needs are already being addressed, and what approaches have worked in the past. (You can record your findings on Worksheet 2B, questions 5 through 7, page 136.)

Consider the following questions as you assess community resources.

1. **What are other funders doing?**

   Find out if other funders support capacity building in the community, what kind of assistance they provide, and what they are learning. Examine whether there are gaps in assistance. Think about whether there would be added value if you teamed up with other grantmakers. If another funder is providing adequate support to a particular area, you might want to focus your efforts elsewhere. For example, when the David and Lucile Packard Foundation started its Emerging Community Foundation Initiative, the James Irvine Foundation focused its support on small and midsize community foundations and funded the League of California Community Foundations to provide capacity building assistance to community foundations throughout the state.

2. **What capacity building resources exist in the community?**

   Learn who is providing capacity building services and resources in the community. (See the sidebar on page 23, Capacity Building Providers.) Do they serve a particular industry or provide services related to a particular organizational area? Find out whether enough resources are available and whether they are strong or variable in quality. Do capacity building providers have the necessary skills and knowledge? Do they collaborate with each other or make referrals to others with stronger skills?

3. **What are promising capacity building approaches?**

   Ask nonprofits, capacity builders, and other funders what capacity building efforts have been used in the past—locally, nationally, or internationally—that seem to be especially successful. The Council on Foundations, Grantmakers for Effective Organizations, and Grantmaker Evaluation Network web sites and conferences are good places to begin learning about others working on similar issues (see Appendix B).

This task led you through a systematic process of taking stock of nonprofit and community needs and resources. This information will prepare you for making strategy decisions during the remainder of your planning process. You are now ready to begin the third task within Step 2.

Methods for Assessing External Needs and Resources

Many different methods can be used to collect information, depending on how thorough and objective you want to be, and how much time and resources you have available. You have three choices to make.

1. **How to collect information:** Consider surveys, focus groups, and interviews involving nonprofit or community leaders, other stakeholders, funders, and capacity building providers. Site visits to other funders or management support organizations will yield valuable information. You might also want to conduct a literature review. Usually a combination of methods works well.

2. **Who will collect information:** Staff from your organization can undertake the discovery process, or you can hire an outside consultant or research group to gather the information. Often a mixture of the two is most effective, ensures some degree of objectivity, informs staff about the issues, and begins to build relationships and your organization's profile in the process.

3. **Who will summarize and analyze information:** You will end up with a great deal of raw data that will need analysis and interpretation to make it useful for decision making. Again, often a combination of external and internal people works well.

Reach out broadly when conducting needs assessments. The New York Community Trust and United Way of New York City surveyed over 180 nonprofit organizations in New York City in 1993 to determine their management assistance needs. This study revealed that fundraising, marketing, and strategic planning were the most pressing issues.[21]

Be sure to update needs assessments as the operating environment for nonprofits shifts. In 2000, the New York City HIV Health and Human Services Planning Council assessed the management development needs of community-based organizations in New York that serve people with HIV and AIDS, considering recent changes in welfare reform, managed care, and immigration policies. The study revealed that organizations needed most support in the areas of board development, financial management, and information systems.[22]

Look at both the supply and demand side to determine interrelationships and gaps. In 1999, the Cleveland Foundation investigated how it might work more effectively to strengthen the community's nonprofit infrastructure. It identified nonprofit needs and challenges; assessed the strength of capacity building resources; and learned from other grantmakers. The foundation concluded that there was a mismatch between what nonprofits needed and the services available among providers, especially in the areas of computer/MIS consultations, program evaluation, and change-management consultation where there was greater need than availability.[23]

Task Three: Acknowledge your organization's values and assumptions

During Task Three, you will identify organizational values and assumptions. These may affect what capacity building goals you commit to and how you will achieve them.

Most organizations have a broad set of values and operating assumptions that are deeply held and guide their actions. Sometimes these are explicit, sometimes not. They usually emerge later in a planning process when alternative courses of action are being considered, or even during implementation, after program development has occurred. When value issues are identified too late, they can sometimes bring efforts to an abrupt halt or cause you to rethink your approach. It is useful to at least begin to identify values and assumptions early in the planning to inform decisions about goals, strategies, and resource allocation.

Values can vary widely and are often grounded in an organization's history and community needs. For example, the Headwaters Fund was started by people with inherited wealth who grew up in the 1960s in families with a culture of philanthropy. Its activist-controlled grantmaking and direct capacity building work focus on addressing the root causes of social problems and strengthening grassroots leadership. The organization values social, economic, and racial justice.[24]

You may also hold values about the role you prefer to play in your relationships with grantees and in the community. Your role preferences may guide your selection of capacity building strategies, or they may need to be altered to engage in capacity building work.

Being clear about your organization's values and assumptions as you commence capacity building work will help you make wise strategy choices, allow you to be more open in your dealings with the community, enhance your relationship with constituents, and encourage disclosure from grantees and other stakeholders. But how do you identify your organization's values?

Three actions are involved in clarifying your organization's values related to capacity building work:

1. Identify your organization's values

2. Test and confirm values

3. Determine implications for capacity building strategies

Each action is described below. You can use Worksheet 2C: Acknowledge Your Values and Assumptions on page 137 to guide you through these actions.

Identify your organization's values

Start by generating an initial list of your organization's deeply held values and beliefs. Many value statements can be found in mission statements, strategic plans, program descriptions, grant guidelines, historical documents, and other organizational materials. But don't stop there.

You may need to articulate values that haven't yet been written down. Ask yourself *why* you are thinking about investing in capacity building. It may be because you believe that nonprofits are stretched so thin that they aren't focusing enough on program quality. Or you may think that you really could have greater impact with limited grant dollars by investing deeply in a few really strong organizations. Or you may assume that mainstream organizations aren't serving populations most in need, and you want to invest in start-up capacity building efforts with grassroots organizations. Perhaps you think that nonprofits need to apply private sector practices to their operations and become more businesslike. If you believe that grantmaking is like investing in a venture, you might see capacity building as a way to maximize your return on investment.

Each of these reasons illustrates a different kind of value, as described in the sidebar Five Kinds of Values. Read the sidebar and think about how your organization relates to each of these five categories.

You may want to solicit ideas from other staff within your organization, either individually or in a group setting. Brainstorming implicit or explicit values behind the work you do can lead to a lively group discussion. Your aim initially isn't to narrow the list. You want to generate as many ideas and opinions about values that guide your organization's work as possible. In the next action, you will narrow the list and confirm your values.

Five Kinds of Values

Recognizing the kinds of values your organization holds can help you determine capacity building goals. Here are five kinds of values.

1. Values and assumptions regarding ***ends***, often contained in mission statements. Or you could ask, Build capacity for what? This type of value will directly inform the goals and objectives you define in Step 3. For example:

   - Support innovation, expansion, and replication of effective youth development programs

   - Ensure high-quality artistic development

   - Reduce poverty

2. Values and assumptions regarding ***the kind of capacity it is important to build, or the meaning of organizational effectiveness work***. These values will help determine your overall approach. For example:

   - Strengthening grantees' self-sufficiency is necessary for their survival

   - Helping nonprofits clarify and measure outcomes will enhance the quality of services and programs

   - Building neighborhood organizing capacity will enhance the quality of life for residents

3. Values and assumptions regarding ***program imperatives or constraints***. These values will influence program strategy and design. For example:

   - Create programs and then spin them off

   - Fill gaps, instead of duplicating what is already being done

   - Provide a unique, high-quality, and high-profile program

   - Do not provide general operating support grants

   - Preserve foundation's endowment

   - Increase return on investment

   - Partner with other funders

4. Values and assumptions regarding ***who will be served***. These values will determine your identification of a target audience. For example:

   - Strengthen our current grantees

   - Support a few strong organizations long term

   - Reach as many organizations as possible

   - Strengthen organizations serving new immigrant groups

5. Values about your ***preferred role in grantee and community relationships***. For example:

   - Maintain an engaged style of working with grantees

   - Stay hands-off, allowing grantees to determine their own goals and methods of work

Test and confirm values

You now have a beginning list of values, some of which come from organizational materials, and some of which may be your own or others' ideas. Review this list with key decision makers in your organization.

Determine implications for capacity building strategies

As mentioned, your organization's values will inform your choices about goals and strategies and the allocation of resources. For example, if your trustees want to encourage financial self-sufficiency, then you might choose to concentrate on supporting the development of earned-income ventures among grantees. If your mission promotes achievement of outcomes, you may want to help nonprofits increase their capacity to evaluate programs and track results.

For each of the values you identified, note the implications it may have for your capacity building strategy. When you have finished articulating your values, you are ready to move to Step 3: Set Direction.

Shortcut for Step 3

Step 3: Set Direction can be done quickly, if needed. Start by setting some basic goals and objectives. The strategy selection process can be easy if you narrow your options quickly. If you have limited financial resources or want to build your efforts incrementally, see the section Prioritize and Select Strategies on page 62 for suggestions on choosing some smaller-scale and simple capacity building strategies.

Step 3: Set Direction

In the previous steps, you assessed the needs and resources of your community and the organizations you want to help, as well as your organization's readiness and values. You are now ready to make choices about what you hope to accomplish and the approach you will use to strengthen the non-profit organizations—and ultimately the communities—that you serve.

During Step 3, you will undertake three major tasks:

Task One: Define your goals and objectives

Task Two: Select strategies

Task Three: Commit resources

Worksheets 3A through 3D in Appendix C will guide you through this process.

Task One: Define your goals and objectives

You are ready to define goals and objectives for your capacity building work. Worksheet 3A: Define Your Goals and Objectives on page 138 will help you with this task. (If your goals and objectives are not apparent at this point, you might want to begin Task Two: Select strategies, and articulate your goals and objectives as your strategies become clearer.) Three actions are involved in this task.

1. Establish goals
2. Specify objectives
3. Start evaluation planning

Establish goals

Goals are major outcome statements that define what you are trying to accomplish. Goals articulate the expected long-term results that will be achieved from your capacity building work: If you are successful helping nonprofits build their capacity, what will be different? What impact do you want to have? Agree on expected outcomes with grant recipients at the outset of a grant. Be sure that your goals address community and organizational needs, are achievable, and describe an end result, not an activity. For example, a funder of a four-year initiative might establish a goal to "improve the governance of ten community-based youth organizations in Maple City, in order to enhance their ability to deliver effective services to youth." Because needs and resources vary greatly, initiatives can have a wide range of goals. The sidebar Sample Goals provides examples of goals of capacity building initiatives.

Sample Goals

The following are some examples of funders' goals for capacity building initiatives.

- The Rockefeller Family Fund set up TechRocks as a supporting organization to "encourage and enable foundations, advocacy groups, and leading activists to use technology to achieve their goals, to increase participation from interested constituencies, and to achieve change more quickly than by traditional organizing and advocacy methods alone."[25]

- Nonprofit Enterprise Self-Sustainability Team (NESsT) strives "to help international civil society organizations increase their long-term viability and independence by generating some of their own resources to supplement support from public and private donors."[26]

- The Corporation for Supportive Housing's Capacity Building Program has three goals: "1) to increase the capacity of nonprofit supportive housing providers to produce and manage service-enriched housing; 2) to provide quality supportive services in the context of managed care; and 3) to strengthen the administrative and fiscal operations of the providers in the context of an austere funding environment."[27]

- The James Irvine Foundation-funded Youth Development Resource Project, which was implemented from 1994 to1999, aimed to: "1) build the capacity of youth-serving organizations, their leaders, and staff members to operate effectively and develop youth who will become healthy, able adults participating to the maximum of their ability in society and 2) strengthen the capacity of consultants, management assistance providers, and other professionals to coach and assist youth service organizations in achieving their aim."[28]

- Shatil is a program of the New Israel Fund that provides training and consulting to Israeli voluntary organizations. It aims to "empower the underprivileged with the tools to improve their lives and communities and builds institutions to promote long-term social change."[29]

Specify objectives

For each goal, specify one or two objectives that articulate what needs to be accomplished to achieve the goal over a short duration. Be sure to quantify your targets and link them with deadlines. Objectives need to be precise, measurable, and time bound. For example, "By the end of year one, at least seven out of the ten community-based youth organizations in Maple City involved with the initiative have 80 percent attendance at board meetings and 100 percent board participation in annual giving." As your work proceeds, you will be able to monitor whether objectives are being achieved and revise them if necessary.

Start evaluation planning

Do not wait until you are implementing capacity building strategies to begin your evaluation efforts. Since objectives need to be quantifiable, now is a good time to begin planning how you will measure success during the evaluation. If you have an evaluator on board at this stage, he or she can be involved in specifying objectives, laying out a logic model, and forming strategies. By considering your evaluation approach at the outset, you allow the evaluation to help shape the program design. (You will learn more about evaluation in Step 4.)

After defining your goals and objectives, you are prepared to proceed to strategy selection.

Task Two: Select strategies

In the previous task you defined your goals and objectives. Now, you need to choose the strategies—broad priorities, directions, and activities—for achieving your desired outcomes. Decision makers, such as those on the planning committee if you have one, need to be involved in strategy formation so that they feel a sense of ownership of your choices.

The strategy selection process depends on whether or not you are currently undertaking capacity building strategies. If you are, you may choose to abandon existing strategies that are not working, maintain and refine those that are working well, or embark on innovative ones. If you have a blank slate, you need to decide which new strategies to select.

This task involves three main actions:

1. Consider the range of possible strategy choices
2. Assess strategy alternatives
3. Prioritize and select strategies

International funders will want to refer to Appendix A when considering strategies.

Consider the range of possible strategy choices

Funders can use a wide range of strategies to support nonprofit organizational effectiveness. These are illustrated in Figure 5 on page 58. While some approaches are geared toward providing management assistance to nonprofit organizations, others focus on supporting capacity builders, intermediaries, researchers, and educators, who in turn provide benefits to nonprofits. Most of the strategies involve providing financial resources through grants and loans, but a funder can also provide direct management assistance.

Figure 5 lists seven types of capacity building strategies:

1. Program grants that promote organizational effectiveness
2. General operating support grants
3. Grants specifically to increase organizational effectiveness
4. Capital financing for nonprofits and intermediaries
5. Grant support to capacity builders and intermediaries
6. Grants to conveners, educators, and researchers
7. Direct management assistance

1. **Program grants that promote organizational effectiveness**

   You may integrate capacity building into your organization's regular grantmaking process. You can do this by considering organizational issues when reviewing proposals and making program grants, such as by funding management assistance as a component of a program grant.

2. **General operating support grants**

   Judicious funding for general operations can be a critical driver for organizational effectiveness. General operating support can help nonprofits be adaptive and innovative. It also enables them to invest in much needed infrastructure—such as technology, administrative staff, and operational systems—not usually covered by project and program funding.

3. **Grants specifically to increase organizational effectiveness**

   You can award grants to nonprofits specifically to build organizational capacity through such activities as strategic planning, board development, or staff training. Funding such activities usually complements, rather than replaces, program grants.

4. **Capital financing for nonprofits and intermediaries**

   By providing capital financing to nonprofit organizations, you can help them improve their financial position, institute healthy financial practices, and improve their productivity and performance. There are three types of capital: facilities capital, working capital, and permanent capital. Financing is usually in the form of loans, yet permanent capital financing can be grants.

5. **Grant support to capacity builders and intermediaries**

   You can enhance nonprofit organizational effectiveness by supporting groups that provide capacity building assistance to nonprofits, including nonprofit management assistance and training providers, intermediaries, independent consultants, and private consulting firms. You can subsidize their provision of assistance, provide them with general operating support, contract with them to assist grantees, refer nonprofits to them, and strengthen their own organizational capacity.

6. **Grants to conveners, educators, and researchers**

   You can help build knowledge related to nonprofit organizational effectiveness and develop the skills of nonprofit leaders by funding research, education and training, convening, and peer exchanges.

7. **Direct management assistance**

   A small but growing group of funders is providing management assistance directly to nonprofits. This support includes offering training, providing consulting assistance, making community-wide interventions, and placing funder representatives on nonprofit boards.

Chapter 4: Capacity Building Strategies provides more information on specific strategies.

Figure 5: Capacity Building Strategies

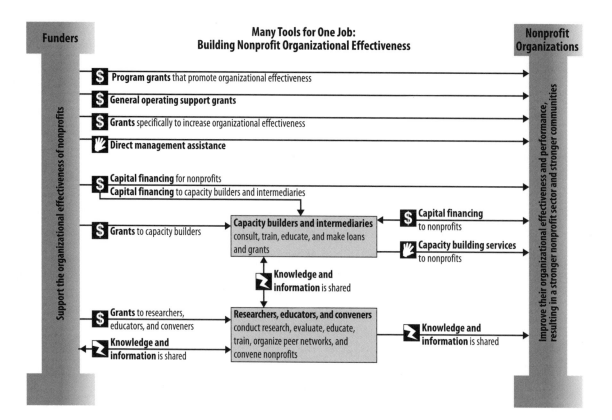

Assess strategy alternatives

Begin by brainstorming possible strategies. In order to begin sorting out your alternatives, encourage thoughtful dialogue about the data you gathered during your previous steps. Your goals and objectives will guide your strategy formulation. Identify strategy options that match what you intend to do, what you are capable of doing, and what is needed and feasible.

Narrow the options in a disciplined manner. The decision makers involved need to agree on criteria for selecting strategies. Some criteria for assessing and choosing strategies could include

- Helps you achieve stated goals and objectives

- Is congruent with your organization's mission, values, and culture

- Addresses a perceived need in the community

- Coordinates with other programs

- Is feasible, fits your organization's readiness and capability, and takes advantage of your organization's competitive advantages and distinctive competencies

- Responds to external needs and resources

- Has adequate funding and human resources devoted to it

- Is acceptable to decision makers and other stakeholders

You may want to assign more importance to criteria that fit especially well with your organization. You might add other criteria that relate to the level of risk or innovation, the flexibility, or the cost-effectiveness of the strategy. Worksheet 3B: Assess Strategy Options on page 139 provides a template for assessing strategy options according to the criteria described above.

Table 1 identifies benefits and limitations of each of the strategies outlined in Chapter 4 and may help you weigh the various alternatives. Note that these are possible benefits and limitations. You may want to add others or consider these in light of your particular situation.

Table 1: Benefits and Limitations of Capacity Building Strategies

Strategy	Benefits	Limitations
1. Program grants that promote organizational effectiveness	● A relatively easy, incremental approach if you want to start small and simple. ● Program grantee performance can be enhanced by improving its organizational management and governance. ● By integrating capacity building into your regular grantmaking, you avoid the possibility of having a "special initiative" become marginalized.	● If program officers are not knowledgeable about organizational development, they may not be able to effectively integrate capacity building into regular grantmaking. ● This approach risks being shallow, not allowing for targeted capacity building efforts.
2. General operating support grants	● Through general operating support you address the most pressing infrastructure needs for many nonprofits. ● This approach allows nonprofits to innovate, improve quality, or expand successful programs. ● This approach provides a vehicle for rewarding and investing in nonprofits that are producing the strongest impact in your priority areas.	● Determining the "ideal" amount of investment to spur performance is challenging. ● It can be difficult to demonstrate the connection between operating support and program outcomes.
3. Grants specifically to increase organizational effectiveness	● Direct grants to nonprofits for capacity building allow nonprofits to manage their own development process. ● Direct grants can easily be tailored to the unique needs of each organization. ● This is a flexible strategy, allowing you to expand or contract your financial commitment as your circumstances change.	● Because nonprofits define and manage their own capacity building, you may need to negotiate the focus of work if your assessment of needs differs from the nonprofit's assessment. ● Direct grants may require a different time table than your normal grants cycle.

4. Capital financing for nonprofits and intermediaries	○ By providing capital financing to nonprofit organizations, you can help them gain access to capital, improve their financial position, institute healthy financial practices, and, ultimately, improve their performance. ○ By lending money, you can stretch your financial resources without depleting them.	○ Lending money can be more complicated than simply awarding a grant, especially if the funding organization staff is not skilled in credit analysis and loan monitoring and administration. ○ Nonprofits need some basic capacity to borrow money; a poor decision about a loan to a nonprofit without comprehensive planning can end up hurting the nonprofit organization.
5. Grant support to capacity builders and intermediaries	○ Through direct funding of capacity builders and intermediaries you can increase the likelihood that quality resources and assistance are available to support nonprofits. ○ This approach builds a stronger nonprofit infrastructure available to all nonprofits. ○ Direct funding assists with knowledge capture and transfer between organizations.	○ The indirect nature of these grants makes impact difficult to link with your other program areas. ○ Requires skill in assessing which capacity building providers to invest in.
6. Grants to conveners, educators, and researchers	○ By funding knowledge development, delivery, and exchange, you can help nonprofit leaders gain access to tools, develop skills, and learn from each other about nonprofit management and governance. ○ Training and peer exchanges can complement other approaches, such as intensive one-on-one consulting. ○ This approach helps build the capacity of the entire nonprofit sector.	○ This approach is more indirect and is not likely to result in short-term, direct benefits to nonprofit organizations.
7. Direct management assistance	○ With sufficient time investment, skilled assistance, and nurturance of trust, this approach can result in close, mutually vested relationships and positive outcomes. ○ This approach enables a funder to provide coordinated funding and capacity building assistance during a long-term engagement with a grant recipient.	○ It is very difficult to build genuine trust between a nonprofit and a funder who also serves as a capacity builder. ○ Without staff who are knowledgeable about capacity building and have trusting relationships with grantees, this approach can be intrusive and harmful for the nonprofit organizations.

61

Prioritize and select strategies

After assessing each possible strategy, prioritize them. Now you need to make some choices. Select strategies that will best help you achieve your objectives, build on your strengths, and take advantage of opportunities.

For example, if you are new to capacity building or are a small funder with limited financial resources, you might want to start small and simple. Some easy initial strategies might be to build capacity building into your program grants, make general operating support grants, convene grantees for workshops on technology or evaluation, or develop a list of capacity building resources in the community for grantees to access.

If you are aiming to reach a large number of nonprofits and do not have substantial financial resources to commit to the effort, choose a leveraging strategy that builds on other resources and partnerships to extend your impact. If creating or maintaining close relationships with your grantees and community is a high priority, then your approach needs to be engaged, rather than hands-off. If you want to focus on building the capacity of the nonprofit sector, instead of a specific set of nonprofit organizations, select a strategy that supports capacity builders, researchers, or educators. If your organization has skilled consultants on staff and there is a shortage of high-quality management assistance providers in your community, you may choose to provide consulting services directly to nonprofits while investing to improve the quality of other available assistance.

If you intend to provide support to capacity builders, researchers, educators, or conveners, or provide direct management assistance, Worksheet 3C: Select Strategies on page 140 will help you think about possible approaches.

Assistance sometimes needs to be tailored to a nonprofit organization's programmatic niche—human services, community development, education, health care, arts and culture, religious, or environmental. While some principles and practices regarding nonprofit management and governance apply across industries in the nonprofit universe, each field has different circumstances and specialized knowledge.

Remember that you do not have to choose just one strategy. Frequently, a combined approach is the best course of action. For example, some management support organizations have found that facilitating peer exchanges of nonprofit leaders and then following up with one-on-one consulting is a particularly effective approach. Sometimes focusing on one or two highly concentrated strategies or a specific set of nonprofits is the best way to maximize impact. If you select more than one strategy, try to prioritize them and articulate how they relate to each other.

Make sure that the strategies you choose and the resources you commit will enable you to reach your expected outcomes. For example, you cannot expect vastly improved leadership and organizational transformation to result from a $3,000 board retreat.

Before you start implementing your strategies, consider the level of resources that will be needed to achieve your goals and strategies and obtain commitment from your organization. The following task will help you make resource commitments.

Task Three: Commit resources

Funders have varying levels of financial and other resources to commit to organizational effectiveness and community capacity building. The amount of resources *available* will be determined, in large part, by your organization's assets and degree of commitment to capacity building. The amount of resources *required* will depend on the strategies that you select. Your job is to find the right match between these two elements.

At this point, you have facilitated a systematic planning process that included assessment of community needs and resources, examination of your organization's values and assumptions, creation of goals, and strategy selection. You have made choices that will have budget implications. Now two actions remain before you proceed to Step 4:

1. Develop a budget
2. Obtain organizational commitment

Develop a budget

Cost out your proposed capacity building strategy for at least a three-year period. As part of your budgeting, you need to decide more specific operating assumptions and funding policies that fit your strategy, such as:

- What will be your grant parameters, including the number of grants you expect to make and the average size of a grant?

- Will you make multiyear grants? If so, will you pay out the full amount up front or in stages?

- Will you provide direct management assistance through your own staff? If so, what volume of service do you expect to offer, what staffing level will be needed to do this, and how much will it cost?

- What staff or independent contractors will be needed to implement your strategy?

- What communications tools—community meetings, written materials, or web site enhancements—will be needed to launch your effort?

- Will your foundation need to engage in its own internal organizational effectiveness effort? What resources will be required to do this?

- What do you want to learn about the outcomes or impact of the work?

- What will it cost to evaluate your program? (See Step 4: Take Action and Evaluate.)

- Will you convene grantees for peer learning, training, or other activities?

Use Worksheet 3D: Commit Resources on page 142 to record your budget assumptions. Most funders have well-established budgeting formats and protocols that they regularly use, so a budget template is not included in this book. The sidebar So How Much Does Capacity Building Cost? on page 66 will help you develop a budget.

Obtain organizational commitment

Obtain organizational commitment to your capacity building plan and budget. This is a significant step for your foundation, whether you are initiating a capacity building effort or retooling or expanding an existing one. Make sure that your organization fully understands what capacity building is, how it will enhance the impact of your program grants, and how it will strengthen your role in the community.

Once you have obtained commitment, you are ready to launch your capacity building venture. Step 4: Take Action and Evaluate will help you design and implement ongoing evaluation to help you measure your success and learn from your experience.

So How Much Does Capacity Building Cost?

It *really* depends. Since there are so many variables involved, there is no set formula for determining exactly what different capacity building approaches cost. Following are examples of costs from actual capacity building strategies, including grants for individual organizations and multiyear initiatives involving many nonprofit groups. These strategies range from virtually free to many millions of dollars. Capacity building can cost no more than some donated time, and up to and beyond the resources of your foundation.

- The Rinconda Ventures Foundation, based in San Francisco, manages a team of about fifty volunteers who provide ad hoc consulting for **free** to grantees that are start-up ventures in disability rights.[30]

- The Mary Reynolds Babcock Foundation has made grants of **$3,000** to **$5,000** to help nonprofits with such pressing needs as upgrading financial systems or getting a facilitator for a board retreat.[31]

- The New York Foundation has a small grants pool for technical assistance through which it awards grants from **$500** to **$7,500** to enable grantees to cover the costs of time-limited, hands-on help for such services as fundraising, special events implementation, technology support and assistance, and public relations.[32]

- The Nonprofit Management Fund in Milwaukee awards grants from **$500** to **$10,000** to support management assistance consulting for nonprofit organizations in such areas as board development, planning, fundraising, financial management, technology, human resources, and marketing.[33]

- The Eugene and Agnes E. Meyer Foundation makes grants up to **$10,000** to current grantees for financial management, governance, and organizational assessment capacity building.[34]

- The David and Lucile Packard Foundation awarded a median grant size of **$40,330** in 2000 to program grantees to provide capacity building resources to enhance their effectiveness.[35]

- The Roberts Enterprise Development Fund invests **$100,000** to **$125,000** into social service organizations to help them hire enterprise managers and develop business plans for social ventures.[36]

- The Organizational Capacity Grant Initiative—funded by the Peninsula Community Foundation, the Charles and Helen Schwab Family Foundation, and the Sobrato Family Foundation—awarded **$125,000** over three years to sixteen social service organizations to strengthen their management and governance.[37]

- The Edna McConnell Clark Foundation makes general operating support grants of approximately **$250,000** to leading youth-serving organizations.[38]

- The Hartford Foundation for Public Giving plans to award grants of up to **$300,000** over a three-year period to assist midsize multiservice agencies engaged in a special initiative to strengthen their internal capacity.[39]

- The Edyth Bush Charitable Foundation invested **$750,000** to establish the Philanthropy and Nonprofit Leadership Center at Rollins College in Florida.[40]

- The Bush Foundation operates the Regional Arts Development Program, a five-year initiative with about **$1.5 million** in general operating grants annually to sixteen arts organizations. Grants range in size from $45,000 to $400,000 per organization.[41]

- The Corporation for Supportive Housing awarded **$2 million** in 1997 to ten organizations in New York City to develop their management and financial infrastructure.[42]

- The James Irvine Foundation invested **$4.3 million** in the Youth Development Initiative, a five-year program to strengthen the management and organizational capacity of twenty-two youth-serving organizations.[43]

- The William and Flora Hewlett Foundation provided **$6.76 million** in general operations support to 180 arts organizations in 1998.[44]

Step 4: Take Action and Evaluate

You are launching your capacity building effort. This is an exciting time—soon you will see your assessment and planning come to fruition. You are creating a new relationship with your community, and you will potentially have greater impact on the long-term effectiveness and viability of the nonprofits and communities you serve. Step 4: Take Action and Evaluate guides you as you carry out your new capacity building efforts.

There are two tasks within Step 4:

Task One: Implement strategies

Task Two: Evaluate your efforts

Task One: Implement strategies

Implementation is simple to describe—and much more difficult to carry out. First, you must develop action plans for accomplishing each strategy. The work plan should spell out specific tasks, who is responsible for completing them, their expected duration, and the resources needed. Involve those who will do the work in developing these blueprints for action. Worksheet 4A: Implement Strategies on page 144 includes a series of questions to help you develop detailed plans for implementing each strategy you chose in Step 3.

A good plan needs artful communications. Whether this is a new effort or a retooling of an existing initiative, be sure to keep key people within your organization, and external stakeholders, informed of progress, successes, and challenges.

Remember that the real work begins *after* you make a grant or select a strategy. Chapter 4: Capacity Building Strategies describes in detail ways to implement the various strategies. To be sure your plans are working, monitor your progress regularly. The next task, evaluation, will help you find out

Shortcut for Step 4

If, in keeping with previous shortcuts, your strategies are clear-cut and limited, your work plan and implementation can be straightforward. To keep evaluation simple, begin by articulating what you are building capacity for and agreeing with the grantee on expected outcomes. If your funding organization does not have evaluation expertise and cannot afford to hire an evaluator, at least monitor the progress of the grant, ask the grant recipient to assess the grant itself, and be reflective about your work. Ask yourself Were the outcomes achieved? If not, why? In this simple manner, you can learn something about what resulted from the investment and apply lessons learned to other efforts.

if you are achieving your goals and objectives and determine what strategy changes and resource reallocations are needed.

Task Two: Evaluate your efforts

Your work is not complete after dedicating resources for your strategies and implementing them. Now you need to evaluate your capacity building effort, a process that should have begun when you set your goals and objectives in Step 3 and agreed on expected outcomes with the grantee.

Evaluating capacity building can be difficult. It is hard to develop measurements for assessing organizational effectiveness and management assistance success. And linking capacity building interventions to ultimate social impact is not easy. Even the notion of capacity building carries problems; it is vague, and there are major obstacles in showing a relationship between increased capacity and improved outcomes. Given these barriers, it is not surprising that funders and management support organizations have performed little rigorous evaluation of their capacity building efforts. What has been done has focused more on customer satisfaction and on process than on outcomes.

Yet many compelling reasons exist to thoughtfully evaluate your efforts. Systematic evaluation helps your organization measure the use of resources and results and be more accountable. Evaluation findings support program planning and implementation and can help you decide whether to devote more or fewer resources to a particular grantee or initiative. Evaluation also generates new knowledge and enables the discovery of what works, for whom, and in what circumstances. Finally, it allows grant recipients to learn from their efforts, make midcourse corrections, and articulate the value of their work.

You might need to find an evaluator to help you do this work. Even without a paid consultant, you can still develop the skeleton of an evaluation work plan. To do this, you need to take four actions:

1. Determine who will conduct and participate in the evaluation

2. State general evaluation questions and potential success indicators

3. Develop an evaluation work plan and implement evaluation methods

4. Use and share the evaluation results

What follows is the information you need to stay on task. It is not sufficient information for you to conduct all aspects of your own evaluation, unless your organization already has an evaluator on staff.

Determine who will conduct and participate in the evaluation

Most funders monitor their supported activities by requiring grant recipients to submit progress reports and then reviewing the submitted materials. You might want to go beyond monitoring and conduct more in-depth evaluation. Evaluations can be conducted by foundation staff, external consultants, or grant recipients. Some funders have evaluators on staff, or they regularly work with particular evaluation consultants. Some funders include, as part of the grant, funding for the grantee to contract for its own evaluation. Others specifically require outside assistance as a way to ensure that the evaluation is objective and its design, methodology, data collection, and analysis are sound and valid. An outside evaluator can often dig deeper with a nonprofit grantee than it might be appropriate for a funder to do.

Keep in mind that external evaluations, especially those driven by funders, may prove threatening to grantees. Grant recipients may fear revealing information about sensitive organizational issues to you and the evaluator. At the outset, it is important for all parties—funder, capacity builder, evaluator, and grantee—to explicitly agree about what information can be shared and with whom.

Above all, evaluation should be useful. Encourage grantees to evaluate their capacity building activities for their own purposes. You may need only to be informed of the process, as appropriate. For example, the Eugene and Agnes E. Meyer Foundation's Management Assistance Fund requires grant recipients themselves to assess their activities that are supported by the foundation's funding.[45] Once grantees see the value of evaluation in relation to fulfilling their missions, they will be more likely to institutionalize the evaluation process and incorporate the findings into their work.

State general evaluation questions and potential success indicators

When you are evaluating capacity building, remember to ask Capacity to do what? and have the answer inform how you measure success. It is easier to design an evaluation if the objectives of a grant, initiative, or funded activity are clear at the outset. The objectives you defined in Step 3 are the building blocks of your evaluation. Carefully craft the questions you want addressed in the evaluation; good questions lead to good answers. (If you create a logic model as described later in this chapter, it can be a superb framework for generating questions; see page 77 for more information.) Then, choose indicators of success for each question, and identify some sources of the necessary data. Work with stakeholders to identify the types of evidence you need.

Worksheet 4B: Create an Evaluation Design on page 146 will guide you through this process. It is helpful for your planning group to work through the questions on the worksheet, even if an outside evaluator will be doing the work, because you will clarify your evaluation goals. Table 2 shows a sample of Worksheet 4B, so that you can see how one organization created its evaluation design.

Table 2: Sample Evaluation Design for a General Operating Support Program

Evaluation Questions	Indicators	Information Required	Data Collection Methods
What critical questions do you want to answer?	*What will indicate success for the evaluation questions?*	*What is the source of the information you need?*	*What tools will you use to collect the information you need?*
Question 1: To what extent did the organizations receiving general operating support grow and improve their managerial and governance capacity?	- Scale of programs increases and more clients are served - Board participation increases so that 90% of trustees make an annual contribution and, on average, 75% attend board meetings - New managers are hired - Management systems are improved - Decision-making process is enhanced	- Reports on quantity and quality of client services - Nonprofit managers and board members - Board minutes - Staff meeting notes - Annual grant progress report	- Review organization's documentation of program activity and board meeting attendance and activity - Interviews with trustees and staff members - Staff survey
Question 2: To what extent were the organizations able to build unrestricted income and net assets as a result of the general operating support?	- Unrestricted income and net assets increase by 20% during the grant period	- Nonprofit executives and financial management staff - Audited financial statements	- Analysis of financial performance - Interviews with board and staff members

Develop an evaluation work plan and implement evaluation methods

Your grant and program objectives, available financial resources, and capacity building strategy influence what, when, and how to evaluate. Estimate the potential costs and benefits of getting certain evaluation data—and remember that certainty in evaluation is expensive. After articulating your evaluation questions and determining how you will measure success, develop an evaluation work plan that specifies evaluation methods. If you are using an outside consultant, develop the plan with the consultant. The work plan should designate how and when strategies and outcomes will be assessed and the cost breakdown for each evaluation method.

Determine the tools you need to collect the information. By employing a combination of tools, you can reliably measure both quantitative and qualitative progress toward goals. Quantitative techniques such as surveys frequently use standardized measures that fit diverse opinions and experiences into predetermined response categories. Qualitative methods—such as focus groups, interviews, and case studies—provide greater depth and detail.

Use and share the evaluation results

The planning process described in this chapter is cyclical. Use the evaluation findings to determine what worked, what did not, and why, and then start a new round of planning, refine your goals, improve your grantmaking, and enhance your capacity building impact. Keep in mind that evaluation should be an ongoing, rather than a one-shot, process. Periodic evaluations clarify which activities are getting results or proving unproductive, which strategies need to be refined or abandoned, which evaluative systems need to be improved, and which unforeseen challenges or benefits have occurred.

By sharing results of evaluations, you can help others in the field learn from your experience, sidestep potential pitfalls, and avoid reinventing the wheel. Evaluations can help determine what capacity building efforts work best. As a result, they help you dedicate support to promising approaches and they enable capacity builders to improve their services.

Issues and techniques in evaluating capacity building

Unlike the other tasks described in this chapter, evaluation is usually not a do-it-yourself activity. For that reason, it is important that you, your evaluator, and your grantees consider the following three issues and techniques in evaluating capacity building:

1. Evaluation can be multilayered

2. Different capacity building strategies require different evaluation approaches

3. Logic models can guide your evaluation

Evaluation can be multilayered

Evaluation can be conducted on many levels. At a basic level, an evaluator can simply count numbers, duration, and satisfaction—how many individuals and groups use the capacity building services for what duration and how satisfied they are. (This is often the extent of evaluation conducted by funders and grantees.) Moving deeper, the evaluator can assess the quality of the capacity building strategies through participant ratings, comparison with research-based practices, and expert observation. To go even deeper, evaluators can attempt to determine what participants learned, how they applied the knowledge, and how they changed their behavior. Ultimately, evaluation can determine the long-term impact on the organization and its clients and community. Table 3: Continuum of Capacity Building Evaluation illustrates this broad range of evaluation for training and consulting activities.[46]

The ultimate goal of most funders is to effect organizational change that leads to improved services and stronger communities. But assessing impact becomes increasingly difficult as one goes from the organizational level to the community level. Thus, it is important to define feasible outcomes that can be measured precisely in a cost-effective way.

Table 3: Continuum of Capacity Building Evaluation

Evaluation Level	Attendance, Usage, or Participation • Number of participants and organizations served and engagement duration	Quality of Service • Degree of program excellence	Cognitive Change • Learning or knowledge acquisition	Affective Change • Shift in attitude or emotion	Behavioral Change • Altered behavior
Evaluation Questions Addressed	• How many and what types of people and organizations used the services, which services did they use, and what was the extent of their usage?	• To what extent do the services reflect best practices and current knowledge? • How satisfied were participants with the services? What did they like and dislike about them?	• What did the participants learn as a result of the capacity building activities, and how did they do so?	• To what extent and how have the attitudes and beliefs of participants, staff members, or community members changed regarding the problem or issue being addressed?	• To what extent and how did the participants, organization, or communities apply what was presented during training sessions and advised during consulting engagements? What have they done differently?
Evaluation Methods	• Counting, documenting, and describing participants' characteristics and usage rates	• Identification of best practices and determination if programs incorporate them • Direct observation of service • Customer satisfaction surveys • Exit interviews with participants after engagements	• Observation of training and consulting process • Interviews and surveys of participants about self-reported learning (including pre- and posttest or comparison group studies)	• Self-perception surveys (including pre- and posttest and comparison group studies) • Focus groups, interviews, and participant observation	• Interviews, surveys (including pre- and posttest and comparison group studies), and focus groups with participants and their colleagues

Activity (the capacity building process, such as training or consulting)	Short-Term Outcomes (the direct result of capacity building interventions on individual participants)

Less meaningful · Easier to measure · Shorter term

Organizational manage-ment and governance	Programmatic (organizational level)	Programmatic (organization's clients' level)	Community
• How did overall orga-nizational management capacities (i.e., governance, leadership, management, fundraising, human resource development, financial man-agement, communication, community outreach, etc.) improve as a result of the ca-pacity building engagement?	• In what ways (directly, indirectly, or both) was the quality of pro-grams and services improved? • In what ways was program capacity increased (scale, reach, or extent of impact on target population)?	• What cognitive, affective, and be-havioral changes have constituents shown as a result of receiving programs and services? • How have the organization's constituents' lives improved?	• How have nonprofit organizations improved, on the whole, in a given community? How has the performance of nonprofits in tackling community challenges improved? • How have changes in organizational man-agement and governance and program deliv-ery affected the community? • What impact have these changes had on the community? To what extent have community conditions improved?
• Interviews and focus groups with board, staff, community partners, and collaborators • Review of financial and operational data • Monitoring of progress on strategic plan implementa-tion • Administration of organiza-tional assessments (includ-ing longitudinal or pre- and posttest organizational assessments)	• Interviews with staff who deliver programs, especially focusing on their perceptions about the "criti-cal" organizational resources that they needed and did or did not have to support their work • Surveys and focus groups with clients that gather in-depth information regarding what it was about the engagement and organization that led them to feel satisfied or not • Performance information about program operations	• Surveys, focus groups, and interviews with constituents, focusing on out-comes • Observation of constituents • Interviews or focus groups with those in the community who have observed constituents	• Periodic collection of organizational assess-ments of nonprofits in the community • Surveys of all nonprofit organizations in a given community • Review of resource acquisition in a given community (new grants, contracts, individual donations, etc.) through audits or surveys • Monitoring networking/collaboration activi-ties in a community • Review of evaluation data collected by non-profit organizations • Longitudinal community studies to monitor changes in indicators of community health

Long-Term Outcomes (the longer-term outcomes related to the organization, the organization's clients, and the community)

More meaningful · More difficult to measure · Longer term

Different capacity building strategies require different evaluation approaches

How you measure success will depend on the nature of the capacity building work that you are supporting. For example, the techniques used to measure the success of management assistance, general operating support, or provision of working capital are very different.

A funder providing grants for management assistance (or providing the assistance directly) might begin by conducting an organizational assessment of each grantee. (See Assess Organizational Needs on page 91 in Chapter 4.) Then, the funder could work together with the management assistance provider and the grantee to establish specific objectives for progress. After measuring baseline organizational data, the funder would evaluate the status of the organization over time.

The Corporation for Supportive Housing used this approach to evaluate its capacity building program for a set of organizations. It measured indicators for organizational health at the outset and then tracked progress in reaching performance benchmarks throughout the intervention. The evaluator found that the participating nonprofits used strategic plans more, became fiscally stronger, and improved their administrative systems.[47]

Similarly, large general operating support grants can be evaluated by appraising grantees' progress in organizational effectiveness. The William and Flora Hewlett Foundation examines the program strength, community participation, governance and managerial capacity, ability to plan, and fiscal health of performing arts groups that receive general support.[48]

Likewise, when providing working capital or facility loans to a nonprofit group, funders could measure both organizational performance and financial stability. Success indicators might include the ability to pay back the loan, levels of working capital reserves, current liquidity, and earned income. The success of permanent capital investments might be measured by reviewing endowment and reserves growth and, if appropriate, an organization's success in matching the grant.

Logic models can guide your evaluation

Common sense says that a well-run organization will be more likely than a poorly managed organization to operate productive programs, meet its goals, and survive unfavorable changes in the external environment. But precisely what effect do capacity building efforts have on organizational functioning? How do changes in individuals within the organization translate into organizational change? How do these changes affect the provision of services? Finally, what is the impact on the people and communities that depend on those services?

The *logic model* helps bring order to these questions and to the underlying theory—in this case, the "common sense" that a well-run organization will be more effective. A logic model is a pictorial representation of a theory of change—or why and how an initiative will happen. The logic model serves as the evaluation framework from which all evaluation questions, data collection tools, methodologies, and data analysis derive and provides a frame of reference for testing assumptions and having a dialogue about ways to make improvements. This approach begins by spelling out the program's inputs, activities, outputs, and outcomes. (Often this is done by asking the program's key stakeholders.)

Inputs are the resources employed, such as funding, staff, or other stakeholders. *Activities* are what happen during the period being studied, such as training programs offered. *Outputs* describe the direct results of the program efforts, such as the number of people who attended the training. *Outcomes* are the changes the program will help bring about, such as increased performance by the training participants. To provide a context for the program and uncover any biases, you might also want to include a box that states your assumptions. Figure 6: Sample Logic Model shows a sample logic model for a funder that supports an initiative to increase the technology capacity of a set of human service agencies. Worksheet 4C: Create a Program Evaluation Logic Model on page 147 is provided should you wish to develop a logic model for your evaluation.

Figure 6: Sample Logic Model

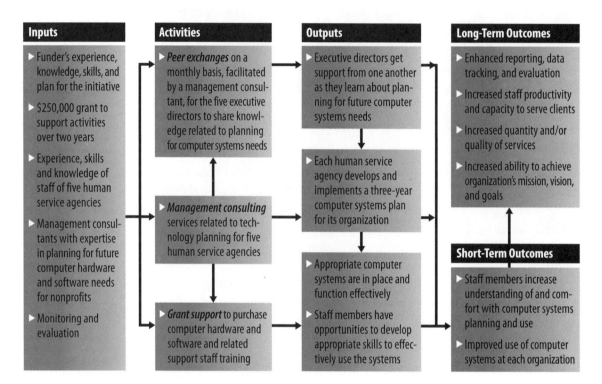

Inputs

▶ Funder's experience, knowledge, skills, and plan for the initiative

▶ $250,000 grant to support activities over two years

▶ Experience, skills and knowledge of staff of five human service agencies

▶ Management consultants with expertise in planning for future computer hardware and software needs for nonprofits

▶ Monitoring and evaluation

Activities

▶ *Peer exchanges* on a monthly basis, facilitated by a management consultant, for the five executive directors to share knowledge related to planning for computer systems needs

▶ *Management consulting* services related to technology planning for five human service agencies

▶ *Grant support* to purchase computer hardware and software and related support staff training

Outputs

▶ Executive directors get support from one another as they learn about planning for future computer systems needs

▶ Each human service agency develops and implements a three-year computer systems plan for its organization

▶ Appropriate computer systems are in place and function effectively

▶ Staff members have opportunities to develop appropriate skills to effectively use the systems

Long-Term Outcomes

▶ Enhanced reporting, data tracking, and evaluation

▶ Increased staff productivity and capacity to serve clients

▶ Increased quantity and/or quality of services

▶ Increased ability to achieve organization's mission, vision, and goals

Short-Term Outcomes

▶ Staff members increase understanding of and comfort with computer systems planning and use

▶ Improved use of computer systems at each organization

This logic model shows the short- and long-term outcomes for activities undertaken to increase the capacity of five human service organizations to plan for and make effective use of computer systems.

Chapter Summary

This chapter began with a set of lessons for you to keep in mind throughout your capacity building work:

- Follow other funders' promising practices
- Do no harm
- Develop clear expectations regarding confidentiality and communication
- Build on nonprofits' strengths
- Remember that one size does not fit all
- Be patient and flexible
- Coordinate efforts with other funders
- Hold your own organization to the same standards you expect of others
- Keep the focus on mission

It then delineated a four-step process—from planning to evaluation—to help you carry out your work.

- Step 1: Plan to Plan
- Step 2: Take Stock
- Step 3: Set Direction
- Step 4: Take Action and Evaluate

Chapter 4: Capacity Building Strategies explains in depth the various strategies you can pursue.

Chapter 4

Capacity Building Strategies

C HAPTER 3 DESCRIBED HOW TO CHOOSE AND CARRY OUT CA-
pacity building strategies that are aligned with your goals, values,
capabilities, community needs, and resources. This chapter explains
seven strategies that you can use to help nonprofits build their capacity:

Strategy 1: Program grants that promote organizational effectiveness

Strategy 2: General operating support grants

Strategy 3: Grants specifically to increase organizational effectiveness

Strategy 4: Capital financing for nonprofits and intermediaries

Strategy 5: Grant support to capacity builders and intermediaries

Strategy 6: Grants to conveners, educators, and researchers

Strategy 7: Direct management assistance

For each strategy, examples are included to illustrate different ways that you
can implement the approach. Some strategies are more complex than others
and thus require more lengthy descriptions. (Funders who work internationally may need to tailor these strategies. Information on the challenges
when building capacity internationally is provided in Appendix A.)

Strategy 1: Program Grants That Promote Organizational Effectiveness

You do not have to create a distinct program to support organizational effectiveness. In fact, you might risk having a "special initiative" become marginalized if it is not part of your main grantmaking efforts. Therefore, consider incorporating capacity building into your organization's regular program grantmaking.

Start by examining how your current program grantmaking encourages or discourages the building of organizational capacity. Ask grantees what your funding organization does that makes it harder for them to manage, such as having idiosyncratic reporting requirements. In other words, determine what you are currently doing that you can *stop* doing to help your grantees.

Even more, you can fund management assistance as a component of a program grant; liberalize rules on indirect costs; include matching requirements; and award multiyear grants to increase organizations' ability to plan and implement program initiatives. Some funders incorporate capacity building support into all of their grants. For example, the Mary Reynolds Babcock Foundation earmarks about 15 percent of the amount of each program grant for organizational capacity building support.[49]

Design your proposal guidelines or application forms to prompt self-assessment about organizational capacity. When composing proposal summaries for trustees to review, consider writing less about the program and more about the organization's management and governance and its capacity to sustain its programs. During the proposal review process, encourage grant seekers to think of capacity building as a legitimate part of running an organization, and encourage or help them to assess their management and organizational condition. Review their strategic (or master or facilities) plans with them, and inquire about their ability to implement them. Ask the executive director to walk you through the organization's audited financial statements, and ask about the organization's history of financial performance. Challenge nonprofits to have staff and organizational development plans and budgets as part of their grant proposals. Expect development goals to be clearly stated, and look for evidence of progress in meeting them. For example, the Edyth Bush Charitable Foundation conducts governance and management reviews for all grants.[50] In addition, the Environmental Support Center has produced guidelines for environmental grantmakers on how to take organizational issues into account throughout the entire grantmaking process.[51]

Program staff may be very knowledgeable about their particular program area, but they may need to learn more about organizational assessment and capacity building. You may want to train your program officers and trustees in areas related to nonprofit governance, management, finance, leadership, and oversight so that they can assess and address organizational capacity needs better. In some cases, especially if your organization provides direct management assistance, you may need to hire new staff members who are experts in these areas. However, not every program officer has to, or should, become an expert in organizational theory. But program officers may need to know enough to recognize signs that an organization may be in trouble or need assistance. They can then encourage the organization to address the issue or call in an expert advisor to help them understand what could be done to strengthen the organization.

Strategy 2: General Operating Support Grants

Most nonprofit organizations agree that their most pressing need is ongoing general operating support. During program expansion or transition, the need for operating support is even more critical. In a constantly changing environment, nonprofits need to be flexible, adaptive, and innovative. Years of "getting by" on program and project grants and inadequate earned income have left many nonprofits with a sorely weakened infrastructure, insufficient administrative staff, inadequate equipment and technology, and vulnerable facilities because of deferred maintenance. Christopher F. Edley, former president of the United Negro College Fund, notes that funders who provide support for programs without funding general operations "insist on feeding us caviar when our schools are starving for rent and bread and water."[52]

Some funders only fund projects that satisfy the funding organization's donors, have easily monitored outcomes, or prevent grantees from becoming too dependent on them. Yet others believe that judicious and intentional funding for general operations is a critical driver for organizational effectiveness. As a 1999 Grantmakers in Health report notes, "With governments cutting back their support for social service and other programs…organizations have few places to turn for resources to sustain their 'bread and butter' activities."[53] And Paul Light, in his book *Sustaining Innovation: Creating Nonprofit and Government Organizations That Innovate Naturally*, points out that "organizations need some slack to innovate."[54]

In addition to general operating support, several vehicles are available to cover costs such as program expansion, facilities maintenance, and innovation. For more information on other options, see Strategy 4: Capital Financing for Nonprofits and Intermediaries on page 95.

Grantmakers in the Arts recently published a booklet, *General Operating Support: A View from the Field*, that describes nine arts funders that share similar philosophies about the value of operating support. These funders wholeheartedly believe that operating support encourages organizational health and long-term sustainability.[55]

Some funders supplement grants for general operations with management assistance. The Twin Cities Local Initiatives Support Corporation (LISC), a community development intermediary, started the St. Paul Fund for Neighborhood Development (SPFND) in 1992 as a multiyear operating support and capacity building program for St. Paul community development corporations (CDCs). Participating CDCs receive an average of $52,000 a year in core operating and management assistance funding.[56]

General operating support can be a powerful tool to assist nonprofits in investing in much needed infrastructure—technology and equipment, administrative staff, internal systems upgrade, financial management capabilities, and a host of other operational and programmatic needs not usually covered by project and program funding. As you plan an operating support program, you will need to consider three main issues:

1. Identity whom to target
2. Determine level of support
3. Build in accountability

Identify whom to target

You may want to first consider the needs of your current grantees when you decide to provide general operating support. Alternatively, you could choose more specific guidelines, such as funding start-up organizations that are meeting a critical community need. In this case, your goal would be to help the organization focus on program development and quality assurance rather than fundraising. Or you might give priority to exemplary programs with potential for replication or increased scale. For example, Broward County Cultural Affairs Council in Florida provides grants for organizations that have been in operation for at least two years to meet general operating expenses associated with the presentation of a regular season of public exhibitions, programs, or performances. Grants range from $8,000 to $65,000 annually.[57]

Determine level of support

You need to determine the right amount of support to avoid either overcapitalization or undercapitalization. Too much, and the organization may not use discipline in its spending decisions. Too little, and the organization may not be able to achieve its desired outcomes.

There is a wide range in the level of general operating support provided by funders and in the methods used in determining the amount. The Mary

Reynolds Babcock Foundation awards grants for general operating support and organization development to grassroots organizations. The foundation offers two consecutive grants: the first averages $30,000, and the second is no more than two-thirds of the first grant.[58]

Build in accountability

Funders who have experience providing general operating support report that it is important to build in concrete performance measures or outcome expectations, monitor progress, and be an engaged partner with the nonprofit. Establishing clear outcomes and making sure the grantee is monitoring and reporting on progress will ensure that your support is well used. If the grantee is successful and the support leads to improved performance, you can reward the grantee's success with extended support to achieve greater performance. If the grantee does not leverage the operating support into greater organizational performance, have a frank discussion with the grantee to determine what obstacles it met, what it learned, and what it will focus on in the future to improve its performance. In this case, you have a clear choice about the extent to which you continue the operating support. Whether the nonprofit has met every performance objective is not as important as whether it is monitoring its own performance, engaged in a learning process, and making adjustments in its operations to adapt to changing circumstances.

Strategy 3: Grants Specifically to Increase Organizational Effectiveness

Awarding grants to nonprofits specifically to build nonprofit infrastructure and increase effectiveness is one of the most commonly used capacity building strategies by funders. This strategy allows nonprofits to manage their own development process and be accountable for results. A funder can tailor this approach to fit its values, goals, and financial resources. Capacity building grants typically complement, rather than replace, program grants.

When you directly fund a nonprofit to engage in capacity building work, it should be up to the nonprofit to select or purchase its own capacity building activities and resources. Grant recipients may utilize their own staff to carry out the capacity building activities or purchase outside assistance from a consultant, facilitator, researcher, or other resource. Nonprofits typically obtain competitive bids from several providers, select their preferred provider, and submit a proposal to the funder outlining their rationale, goals, approach, and costs. Grants are awarded based on criteria established by the funder. The nonprofit manages the relationship with the capacity building providers and arranges terms and payment. The nonprofit grantee reports back to the funder on its success in achieving the outcomes of the project. The time frame for these grants can range from a few months to several years.

Making grants to nonprofits specifically to increase organizational effectiveness is one of the most complex strategies to undertake. Because of this, seven concrete steps are described that will guide you through the choices involved in making these grants:

1. Decide whom to target
2. Select grantees
3. Assess organizational needs
4. Establish grant criteria
5. Determine grant size and cost
6. Consider creating a funder pool
7. Be responsive and flexible

Decide whom to target

You can target grants in several ways, depending on the goals, values, and resources of your funding organization and the needs of the nonprofits or community. Use the categories below as a starting point for thinking about whom to target. You may find that they overlap and that a combination of categories works best for you.

- **Grants to program grantees**

  You can target your capacity building funding to your program grantees. By building your grantees' organizational infrastructure and capabilities as well as their programs, they will have even greater success with program outcomes. At the Surdna Foundation, current and past grantees are eligible to apply for grants to address important management issues that can be handled in a short period of time.[59]

- **Grants to non-grantees**

  You might consider awarding grants to any nonprofit organization within your areas of program focus, whether or not the nonprofit is a current or former grantee. Strengthening the nonprofit sector and nonprofits' ability to become more effective and sustainable is a stand-alone goal of many foundations. For example, the Hartford Foundation for Public Giving operates the Nonprofit Support Program to help improve agencies' operating capabilities.[60] The Otto Bremer Foundation's Organizational Effectiveness Program also awards grants to any nonprofit organization within its geographic and programmatic areas of focus, whether or not the nonprofit is a current or former grantee.[61]

- **Grants to support collaborative or community capacity building efforts**

  You might also choose to strengthen collaborations or community-wide infrastructure. Collaboration can be a powerful strategy for achieving ends that one organization cannot achieve alone. For this reason, many funders encourage collaboration. However, forced partnerships rarely work. It is especially important when working with a collaborative to allow the members of the collaborative to define their own needs and plan their own capacity building strategies.

  Los Angeles Urban Funders (LAUF) is a coalition of twenty-one foundations supporting comprehensive community building in three Los Angeles communities, operating under the umbrella of the Southern California Association for Philanthropy and the Regional Association of Grantmakers for Los Angeles. LAUF helps neighborhoods develop the partnerships, leadership, and strategies necessary to implement improvements.[62] The Common Ground program—operated in partnership with the Boston United Way, the Boston Department of Public Health, and originally the Boston Foundation—helps nonprofits design integrated service systems, addressing problems such as alienation from their constituencies and internal communications.[63]

- **Cluster grants**

  An increasingly common capacity building strategy is to make grants to clusters of nonprofits working in a specific field or serving a particular geography or population. These broad capacity building initiatives have benefit beyond their impact within the participating organizations. By building in opportunities for peer learning and support, they can result in stronger relationships and spin-off collaborative efforts among grantees. They can also result in significant learning about the effectiveness of different capacity building strategies.

  In Silicon Valley, the Peninsula Community Foundation, the Charles and Helen Schwab Family Foundation, and the Sobrato Family Foundation jointly invited sixteen social service organizations to participate in the Organizational Capacity Grant Initiative. The initiative gave each organization a grant for $125,000 for capacity building and allowed each organization to set its own agenda. Grant recipients and funders meet periodically to share learnings and offer feedback to one another. Participants report that the meetings have led to increased trust within the group and a transfer of ideas and strategies between organizations.[64]

  On a broader scale, the Pew Charitable Trusts has focused on working-class, transitional neighborhoods that are on the brink of either stabilizing or deteriorating. Its Neighborhood Preservation Initiative targeted nine cities across the country and provided capacity building support to community development corporations to help them stabilize their neighborhoods. The initiative convened participants across cities for learning, conducted forums, and published a report on challenges facing transitional neighborhoods.[65]

Select grantees

You can conduct an open, competitive application process for capacity building grants, similar to the process you use for program grants. Funders normally allow the applicants to define the kinds of capacity building assistance they need. If you are providing capacity building support to program grantees, consider beginning discussions about capacity building needs when you are talking about the program grant and invite grantees to apply.

You might also choose to strategically select nonprofits in whose futures you want to invest, whether because of growing community needs, highly successful programs, or significant levels of prior program funding. Nonprofits that have been selected as a "good investment" for capacity building report that "they felt special, in some way, for being singled out and invited in to be part of a select group. They were able to use this distinction, even honor, as some sign of being valued, and turn it into access to and cash from other funders."[66]

If you initiate capacity building with a cluster of organizations, you may want to select a diverse group of capacity building grantees, hoping that the nonprofits will learn from each other. Or you could choose grantees with similar characteristics, such as youth-serving agencies or start-ups, hoping to learn valuable lessons about promising practices in that kind of organization.

Selecting grantees requires sensitivity and keen judgment; honest dialogue with each organization is important. You need to recognize when organizations are poised to take the next step in their development, truly committed to learning and growth, and ready to commit the time, energy, and resources needed to successfully manage a capacity building effort. You need to judge whether the organization is truly ready for the possibility of profound change.

Assess organizational needs

Organizational assessments are useful diagnostic tools to ensure that the capacity building focuses on the right issues. Comprehensive assessments also help the organization see all aspects of its own functioning, an invaluable first stage in the learning process. Assessments can identify the organization's assets or strengths on which to build, as well as problem areas that may need attention. They also provide baseline data for evaluation purposes. A comprehensive assessment will help an organization see beyond the immediate concern to core organizational capacity issues that will determine its character, scale, reach, and impact for the future.

Organizational assessment can also help the nonprofit avoid misdirecting energy and investment. Figure 2: Components of Organizational Capacity on page 16 describes six components of organizational capacity: mission, vision, and strategy; governance and leadership; program delivery and impact; strategic relationships; resource development; and internal operations and management. All of these components are important in healthy, high-performing organizations. Nonprofits often have immediate, critical needs for assistance, such as fundraising or marketing assistance. Responding directly to these immediate needs may be exactly what will help the organization strengthen its functioning. But other aspects of the organization, such as goal setting or board development, may need help before fundraising or marketing can be useful. A thorough assessment can give a clear picture of priority areas for development.

Consider funding large capacity building projects in two stages—the first for assessment, and the second for implementation, once the issues are more fully understood. You can also conduct repeat assessments over several years to measure change or progress.

Challenges involved in pre-grant assessments include questions about who administers the assessment, who "owns" the findings, and the difficulty of administering a standardized assessment with different types of organizations working in different industries at different stages of development.

Some examples: The Hartford Foundation for Public Giving offers assessments as a starting point for development of a comprehensive technical assistance plan. The Robin Hood Foundation and the Robert Wood Johnson Foundation both conduct organizational assessments of grantees before providing capacity building support to them. Through contracts with local consultants, Local Initiatives Support Corporation (LISC) conducts in-depth assessment of needs with clusters of community development corporations prior to providing operating support or other funds to improve nonprofit management and governance.

There are many different approaches to organizational assessment. You can encourage grantees to conduct a self-assessment or to retain an organization or program consultant to facilitate the process. Both approaches can work, although many believe that assessments are more objective, and therefore more effective, when done by a third party experienced in working with a range of organizations. Some nonprofit industry associations such as the American Association of Museums require accreditation reviews, which are very comprehensive assessments. Appendix B lists several resources for organizational assessment instruments.

Establish grant criteria

Establish very specific grant criteria for capacity building grants, including the kinds of organizations that can apply, and what can and can't be covered by grant dollars. Some typical criteria that you might consider include

- Grants available only to 501(c)(3) organizations

- Service to a particular constituency, geographic area, or community need, such as community development or homeless shelters

- Certain types of capacity building, such as strategic planning, marketing, or board development

- An evaluation component that will document achievement of specific capacity building outcomes

- Specific threshold requirements, such as having a positive working capital balance

- Demonstration that the organization has obtained competitive bids from potential providers, including proposals that outline objectives, timeline, deliverables, and cost

- Demonstration of support from the organization's leadership—both board and staff

Every funder has different criteria for capacity building grants, depending on its values and goals. Some funders will support only consultation and training costs; others view such things as expanded facilities or upgraded technology to be legitimate capacity building needs. Consider a range of possible capacity building investments, including consultant and facilitation costs, meeting space and refreshments, tuition, site visits, purchase of written resources, travel costs, attendance at conferences, endowment, capital costs, staff salaries, normal overhead costs, and computer purchases.

Determine grant size and cost

It is difficult to determine an average cost for different types of capacity building activities. Costs vary by approach, size of the organization, the nature and complexity of the process, and the number and cost of outside resources used.

Consider two organizations needing to develop stronger strategic plans: One might benefit greatly from an annual planning retreat with facilitation and meeting costs of $5,000. After the retreat its staff and board quickly develop a written summary of their future direction, and they move into implementation with renewed focus and clear priorities. The other organization requires solid research that will help staff and board understand the changing demographics and needs of the organization's audience, and assistance to decide whether and how to reconfigure their programs to meet these needs. For this organization, the investment to help it reach the same outcome—clear focus and priorities for the future—will be considerably more.

A straightforward strategic planning process for a midsize nonprofit can range from $5,000 to $100,000 or more in consultant costs alone. A complex capacity building project that involves major change, such as strategic planning, board development, and marketing assistance, can range from $20,000 to over $200,000. An initial assessment phase for two-phase projects, before specific capacity building goals are established, might cost anywhere from $5,000 to $50,000.

Chapter 3 listed lessons learned by funders engaged in capacity building. One of the lessons, *Remember that one size does not fit all,* applies to questions about cost. In estimating the amount to invest in any one organization, consider its unique needs, whether or not it is likely to succeed with capacity building, and what approach will have greatest potential for success. See the sidebar So How Much Does Capacity Building Cost? in Chapter 3 (page 66) for additional information on costs.

Consider creating a funder pool

In some communities, groups of foundations have pooled funds designated for capacity building purposes. These funding pools then establish criteria governing the use of the funds, and they often establish a community advisory group or a board made up of representatives of the contributing foundations to review applications and make funding decisions. Funds can be targeted in many ways, depending on the contributors' priorities, such as program type (youth-serving agencies), geographic service area (neighborhood, citywide, statewide), constituencies (youth, new Americans, elders, the homeless), size or stage of organizational growth (start-ups, leadership transitions), or other factors. The fund can be administered by one of the contributing foundations or by a third party hired by the collaborative.

The Management Improvement Fund is a special fund of the Saint Paul Foundation that provides financial assistance to nonprofit organizations that need to improve organizational capacity and management capabilities in order to better serve the community. It was established in 1985 with annual contributions from seven local foundations. Average grant size is $11,300.[67]

Be responsive and flexible

Whatever approach you use to provide capacity building grants, be responsive and flexible—responsive in turning around grant requests quickly, and flexible in renegotiating grant uses as the organization learns more about its needs. Nonprofits often feel urgency about capacity building, especially when organizational problems are interfering with their ability to have the desired impact. In fact, the window of opportunity for this kind of investment is often small, since nonprofits are quite skilled at "making do" and usually busy enough without the added time and complication of undergoing a capacity building effort. And often the organizations will start down one path, learn new information, and shift the focus, requiring redistribution of grant funds. The program officer overseeing capacity building grants becomes a critical partner and supporter to the nonprofit.

As you work with your grantees, unexpected opportunities may arise to provide support in addition to the capacity building grants. A frequent request that funders encounter is for help with how to find consultants or other resource people, and how to be a good consumer of consulting services. Many funders have developed a list of available resources in the community, and some conduct occasional workshops on how to locate, hire, and manage consultants. Another opportunity may be to convene grantees who are working on similar capacity building challenges for peer learning and support.

Strategy 4: Capital Financing for Nonprofits and Intermediaries

Nonprofits desperately need capital financing to enhance their organizational health. The Illinois Facilities Fund and Donors Forum of Chicago recently conducted a statewide survey of 501(c)(3) organizations that revealed the precarious financial health of the state's nonprofit sector. A large number of groups surveyed reported deficits, cash-flow problems, negligible cash reserves, and inadequate facilities.[68]

By providing capital financing to nonprofit organizations, you can help them gain access to capital, improve their financial position, and institute healthy financial practices. Capital can also ultimately help them increase productivity, such as by enhancing efficiency through information technology upgrades and improving performance through better management.

There are three types of capital: facilities capital, working capital, and permanent capital.[69] Each is described below. Usually, you would make loans and program-related investments at below-market rates to nonprofits directly or through such intermediaries as the Nonprofit Finance Fund or Corporation for Supportive Housing. In this way, you can stretch your resources without depleting them. Permanent capital financing can be in the form of grants, but different from the sorts of grants described earlier. Permanent capital grants are less like revenues that impact the income statement and more like investments that affect the balance sheet.

Facilities capital

Facilities capital supports the renovation, building, or acquisition of office and program space. Typically, funders provide this support to arts and cultural groups, child care agencies, and human service organizations, which tend to be more real estate intensive than other types of nonprofits. For example, the United Way of Massachusetts Bay, Fleet Bank, Metropolitan Life, and other funders have supported the Child Care Capital Investment Fund's efforts to help child care providers in Massachusetts to improve or expand their physical space.[70] Beware: Although facilities funding can enhance an organization's health, without comprehensive financial and strategic planning, it can end up hurting more than helping if it burdens a nonprofit with unmanageable debt and maintenance costs.[71] Normally, organizations are expected to have a comprehensive facilities plan in place. Capacity building support might combine a grant to cover costs associated with developing a facilities plan and capital assistance.

Working capital

Working capital helps nonprofits cover expenses during low cash flow and provides them with unrestricted, flexible cash to enable them to grow and build their capacity. Working capital can allow an organization to conduct planning, enhance technology, support staff or board development, and start or expand a social purpose business.[72]

The Nathan Cummings Foundation, along with a number of other funders, has supported the Working Capital Fund, a national program designed to strengthen leading midsize cultural organizations that have reached a critical juncture in their institutional development and are actively seeking long-term sustainability of their artistic achievement.[73] Likewise, the Eugene and Agnes E. Meyer Foundation and the Hartford Foundation for Public Giving make cash flow loans to grantees against delayed receivables, either from grants or contracts.[74] Although the loans are made on a quick turnaround basis, cash flow application processes have been designed to support nonprofit board and staff analysis of financial management processes.

The Tiger Foundation's Social Venture Capital Fund supports for-profit enterprises operated by nonprofit organizations that are striving to increase the availability of permanent and transitional jobs for the hard-to-employ. Tiger's capital finances both the development and growth of social ventures. The investments are structured as program-related investments, recoverable grants, and loan guarantees.[75]

Permanent capital

Some funders provide nonprofits with permanent capital, which pertains to endowments as well as the capital reserves that some nonprofit organizations use to invest in housing and business development. The Ford Foundation, for instance, recently launched a $42.5 million initiative, New Directions/New Donors for the Arts, to strengthen the institutional and financial health of arts organizations. The foundation awarded twenty-eight grants, ranging from $1 million to $2.5 million, designated for permanent capital, including general operating endowments, working capital reserves, and endowed funds for artistic programming. Each grant recipient will seek to match its grant on at least a dollar-for-dollar basis with contributions from individual donors.[76]

Strategy 5: Grant Support to Capacity Builders and Intermediaries

Rather than, or in addition to, providing direct support to nonprofits, you can enhance nonprofit organizational effectiveness by supporting groups that provide capacity building assistance to nonprofits. As you learn more about the resources available in your community or field, you will discover great variety in the kinds of providers, their expertise, and organizational affiliations. See the sidebar Capacity Building Providers on page 23 in Chapter 2 for a listing of common types of capacity building providers and intermediaries.

You may find that many communities and nonprofit fields lack well-qualified resource people to help nonprofits. This shortage of qualified resources manifests in many ways, for example:

- Few, if any, resources are available in rural areas and smaller cities.
- In many communities it is difficult to find resources with the skill and sensitivity to work in organizations serving communities of color or new American populations, where language or cultural knowledge is important.
- It can be difficult to find resources with expertise in a particular program area, such as experts in working with museums or with workforce development programs.
- There may be available resources, but the quality of their work is not consistently strong.

In some cases, there are qualified resources, but nonprofits don't know how to find them.

In Step 2: Take Stock, you surveyed capacity building providers in your community or field. Use what you learned to help you select an appropriate strategy to strengthen the capacity, accessibility, or size of the pool of providers.

You can support and strengthen capacity builders and intermediaries in five ways:

1. Subsidize the provision of capacity building assistance

2. Provide general operating support to capacity building organizations

3. Hire capacity building providers to assist grantees

4. Refer nonprofits to capacity builders

5. Strengthen the nonprofit capacity building field.

Subsidize the provision of capacity building assistance

Capacity building organizations are often caught between two strong pressures—to offer high compensation to attract experienced staff with strong skills, and to keep fees low enough to make services accessible to the nonprofits they serve. Because of this dual pressure, provider organizations often have to rely on funders to subsidize service costs to make them affordable to nonprofits.

You can provide general program support to a management assistance provider so that it, in turn, can provide free or low-cost services to the nonprofit groups it serves. If the provider you want to support is a for-profit entity, you need to make an expenditure responsibility grant, which involves ensuring that the funds are spent for charitable purposes, and filing special reports with the Internal Revenue Service.

Sometimes funders will restrict this subsidized support to a particular size or type of nonprofit, such as small community-based advocacy organizations. USAID's Global Bureau Environment Center funds KEMALA, which focuses on building a network of well-informed, technically competent nongovernmental organizations (NGOs) across Indonesia that adhere to conservation-based natural resource management practices. KEMALA helps these NGOs through grants, technical assistance, and information sharing.[77]

If you are in a community without a nonprofit management assistance organization, you may want to consider funding the development of such a service. This can be a major commitment and might be a good opportunity for collaboration with other funders and higher education institutions in your community.

Provide general operating support to capacity building organizations

You can also provide a general operating support grant to a capacity building organization so that it can expand services, improve knowledge transfer capabilities, invest in technology or research and development, improve evaluation of its services, or improve outreach to nonprofits. For more information see Strategy 2, General Operating Support Grants, on page 83 in this chapter.

Hire capacity building providers to assist grantees

You can hire consultants and facilitators directly to conduct organizational assessments or provide a variety of assistance to grantees. Funders often hire consultants to work with grantees, especially when they have invested a substantial sum of money in the nonprofit through program grants and want to make sure that a particular organizational challenge or opportunity is addressed. Usually the funder and the nonprofit will meet with the consultant together to discuss hopes and expectations for the work. The Robert Wood Johnson Foundation assists community-based health and human service organizations in the New York and New Jersey area through the Small Agency Building Initiative. The foundation hires "coaches" who help the groups conduct organizational assessments, identify technical assistance needs, and provide ongoing support.

Contracting directly with providers helps ensure that your needs get met, but raises the question for all parties of who is working for whom. It also may make be difficult for the grantee to feel ownership of the process or develop a trusting relationship with the capacity builder.

Refer nonprofits to capacity builders

Nonprofits frequently report that they don't know how to find capacity building resources—consultants, facilitators, researchers, training programs, or best-practice research. Yet a scan of available resources in those same communities often shows that numerous programs exist to meet the very needs indicated by the organizations. The challenge for many nonprofits is, first, finding a resource to help with a particular issue and, second, finding a resource likely to provide high-quality assistance with the issue.

You can help connect your grantees with high-quality providers through referrals, and you can link them with other sources of information about capacity building, such as web sites, books, or articles on a related subject. You might want to be cautious about recommending resources, but suggesting a few names or providing names of other organizations that have done similar work can be very helpful.

You can also support development of a community-wide resource. For example, the McKnight Foundation funded the Minnesota Council of Nonprofits to develop a searchable database of evaluation consultants. The final product will be rolled into the Minnesota Nonprofit Yellow Pages, a directory of over one hundred consultants, services, and products available to nonprofits.

Strengthen the nonprofit capacity building field

As reliance on capacity builders increases, funders have begun asking, "How can we build the capacity of the capacity builders?" Rather than investing in one particular capacity building organization, you can invest in the development of a broader and more skilled pool of people and organizations qualified to facilitate and guide effective capacity building processes in your community or field.

Depending on the characteristics of the field of capacity builders in your community, and the needs of nonprofits, you might focus on expanding the size or changing the makeup of the field, strengthening and expanding provider skills, investing in research and dissemination of information about best practices, or building robust networks and cross-referral capabilities among providers.

Some funders have already moved in this direction. The Richard King Mellon Foundation funds the Master Consultant Training Program, which is conducted by the Program to Aid Citizen Enterprise and Bayer Center for Nonprofit Management at Robert Morris University in Pittsburgh. According to Peggy Morrison Outon, executive director at Bayer, the program aims to "expand the pool and deepen the skill level of African American and other consultants working with inner city nonprofits." The Frist Foundation in Nashville has initiated numerous field-building endeavors. It was instrumental in starting the Center for Nonprofit Management, a management support organization, and continues to provide operating support. The foundation also started an awards program to raise the visibility and standards of nonprofit management in the middle Tennessee area.[78]

Strategy 6: Grants to Conveners, Educators, and Researchers

There are many ways you can help build knowledge related to nonprofit organizational effectiveness and develop the skills of nonprofit leaders. You can fund research that helps to create and enhance tools, models, and theories to better understand and address nonprofit management and governance challenges. You could also support the dissemination of this knowledge to nonprofit managers and trustees through educational and training programs, as well as consulting engagements. You might provide opportunities for knowledge exchange, through which those working in the nonprofit sector can share lessons and successful practices. These approaches for knowledge development, delivery, and exchange are described below. (The section Capacity Building Activities on page 19 in Chapter 2 has related information on research, education, training, and peer exchanges.)

Research

The academic field of nonprofit management and governance is young and undeveloped and lacks an integrated body of knowledge, common language, and shared priorities. There are many opportunities for funders to identify and help fill in gaps in research. You can support rigorous empirical research on nonprofit organizational issues, including the effectiveness of specific types of capacity building efforts. This research can help answer hard questions, such as What types of management assistance are most suitable for small, community-based groups? or How should the next generation of nonprofit leadership be cultivated? or What kind of interventions will have the greatest impact?

Recently, there have been some attempts to improve research in the field. Foundations such as the Carnegie Corporation of New York and the Charles Stewart Mott Foundation support the Nonprofit Sector Research Fund, which was established at the Aspen Institute in 1991 and strives to enhance both the quantity and quality of nonprofit research. A total of more than $9 million in grants has supported over three hundred research projects.[79]

The research should be practical and results should be disseminated in order to facilitate the utilization of knowledge. The W. K. Kellogg Foundation provided major funding for a three-year study of how to make research a more effective tool to improve the impact of nonprofit organizations in achieving their mission.

Education and training

You can also fund the education and training of nonprofit managers and trustees. Barbara Kibbe explains why the David and Lucile Packard Foundation has provided resources for grantees to pursue their own learning and development: "Nonprofit leaders come to their roles with passion, commitment, and a real depth of understanding in their respective fields. But they rarely possess a thorough grounding in basic management principles and practices. We have tried to increase nonprofit leaders' access to management training programs so that they are better able to cope with the inevitable challenges they will face in the work of managing an organization and leading a staff."[80]

You can support training efforts that take place outside of university settings. The Oklahoma City Community Foundation has brought national trainers to the city to train nonprofit leaders and distributed publications on related topics such as strategic planning and collaboration. Likewise, the Ford Foundation funded a series of workshops on strategic marketing and partnership development with the private sector for sixteen agricultural research groups around the world.[81]

Also consider supporting nonprofit management education programs. There are over 170 colleges and universities in the United States offering nonprofit degree programs or providing courses in nonprofit management.[82] A recent study of nonprofit and philanthropic academic centers found that funding, faculty involvement, university leadership support, and visibility within the field were the most critical factors that contributed to their long-term viability. The report recommended that grantmakers could bolster academic centers by creating endowed faculty positions and convening center directors and leaders so they can share effective approaches with each other.[83] The Jessie Ball duPont Fund gave Rollins College in Winter Park, Florida, a $420,000 grant to help create the Philanthropy and Nonprofit Leadership Center, which will provide management education to nonprofit executives.[84]

In New York City, Citigroup, along with a number of other funders, has supported the Local Initiatives Support Corporation's capacity building program, which began in the early 1990s. This program has enabled community development corporation (CDC) leaders to receive training at Columbia University's Institute for Not-for-Profit Management. The institute's director, Lori Roth, explains why this effort has been effective: "Many CDCs started off as neighborhood visionaries with few resources. But now, many of these groups have staff of over a hundred and manage hundreds of units of housing. To keep their operations running, leadership and advanced business skills are critical."[85]

Convening and peer exchanges

You can also create opportunities for those who work in the nonprofit sector to candidly discuss mutual concerns and learn from one another. These approaches usually require long-term relationships between funders and nonprofits and consistent attention to building mutual respect and trust. In 1980, the Meadows Foundation helped establish the Center for Nonprofit Management in Dallas, Texas, which provides meeting space where nonprofit managers can talk confidentially. The North Star Fund, based in New York City, organizes an annual event to convene grantees for workshops on both program and management issues.

Funders who use cluster grants or capacity building initiatives are finding that convening nonprofits going through similar development processes has benefits beyond the support and peer coaching that participating agencies receive from other grantees. Participants also build important relationships and enter into new joint efforts to strengthen their programs.

Other philanthropies, such as the Mary Reynolds Babcock Foundation, support learning circles and peer exchanges that facilitate active learning and skill building.[86]

Peer learning is a powerful self-directed learning approach. The Greater Milwaukee Nonprofit Institute's Leaders Circle enables six to eight executive directors and senior leaders to meet in a supportive atmosphere once a week for two hours over eight months, guided by a trained facilitator. Participants reflect on personal and organizational goals and values, share feedback with each other, and help solve problems.

Another approach: Grantmakers have provided support to Eureka Communities, which sponsors fellowships for executives of community-based organizations serving children, youth, and families in five cities in the United States. Each fellow pursues specific, structured personal learning goals by taking a sponsored trip to a mentor agency and by participating in a national learning network.

Strategy 7: Direct Management Assistance

A small but growing group of funders provide management assistance directly to nonprofits. Direct support may include training programs, consultation, placing foundation representatives on grantee boards, and community-wide engagements.

The closer you get to providing assistance directly to nonprofits, the more important it becomes to articulate your values, negotiate clear expectations with the nonprofit about communications, clarify the relationship between the capacity building services you provide and the program grants you make, and ensure you have staff with the knowledge, experience, and cultural awareness to work sensitively. Not just any program officer can provide this direct support—this approach requires the funder representative to be knowledgeable about nonprofit management and governance issues and skilled in methods for providing training and consulting assistance. Although this direct involvement can be risky, with sufficient time investment, skilled assistance, and nurturance of trust, the result can be close, mutually vested relationships and positive outcomes.

Training

Many community foundations, such as the Westchester Community Foundation in New York and the Community Foundation for Monterey County in California, operate in-house training programs for nonprofits. These offerings can cover a range of topics, such as the organizational life cycles of nonprofits, governance, or strategic planning.

Consultation

Some funders provide a combination of funding and consulting to nonprofit groups that they support. Consulting effectively with nonprofits with whom you have past, current, or pending funding relationships can be difficult. Such work requires a significant amount of trust, openness, and reciprocity of influence between the nonprofit and the funder who also serves as the capacity builder. As Melinda Tuan, former associate director at the Roberts Enterprise Development Fund (REDF), a fund that helps nonprofits launch and manage profitable enterprises, observes, some nonprofit groups "saw REDF as meddling and were reluctant to talk openly with REDF staff about their challenges…The challenge of building genuine trust in philanthropic relationships is more difficult than many would like to believe."[87]

Some foundations erect a strong "firewall" between staff involved with grantmaking and those who offer management assistance so that capacity building staff do not divulge sensitive information about management issues to program officers. For example, the staff of Shatil, the in-house consulting group at the New Israel Fund, do not share information about grant recipients with program staff, and they each keep separate files on the public interest groups in Israel that the fund supports. This ensures that nonprofits' candor about organizational problems does not jeopardize program funds. As a result, grant recipients are more comfortable disclosing data confidentially with management assistance staff. There are cases in which Shatil consultants determine that, despite ongoing consulting services, the grantee's management and staff are unable to run accountable and effective programs. These cases are referred to the New Israel Fund's executive director for further examination and possible action. Thus, grantmaking and capacity building come together to serve the overall mission of the organization to enhance grantee ability to bring about social change.[88]

On the other hand, the Robin Hood Foundation encourages collaboration between its grantmaking staff and consulting staff, in order to provide coordinated support of its long-term engagement with grant recipients. Robin Hood's grantmaking staff have experience in managing their needs for capacity building assistance. They refer these issues to other foundation staff, most of whom have backgrounds in management consulting, to provide professional services (including pro bono contributions) in support of program grants. Robin Hood recognizes that trust is an essential element to make this approach effective. The foundation assumes that management issues are challenges to be addressed in partnership. It works to develop and sustain trusting relationships through careful screening before awarding a grant, providing long-term funding with flexibility to respond to emerging needs and fostering open communication.

The Seattle-based Social Venture Partners (SVP) makes long-term commitments to grant recipients in the education and children's services fields and consciously works to build trust gradually with them. SVP runs a volunteer model of venture philanthropy in which individual "partners" donate a minimum of $5,000 annually for at least two years and lend their expertise to capacity building projects for grantees in such areas as marketing, technology, and finance. "The first year is about building trust, learning about each other, and accomplishing projects together; it is to show that each party can deliver, and it's about the nonprofit being able to talk about 'broken parts' with the funder," notes SVP Executive Director Paul Shoemaker. He adds: "Most relationships are tactical and project-based in the first year; it is not usually until the second year, with trust and experience built up, in which a more strategic direction can be shared."[89]

Whether or not you choose to have your program staff and consulting staff share information with each other, clarify with grantees how information they divulge will be used. If there is not good faith between the funder and grantee, it will be difficult to work in partnership to address mutual concerns.

Putting a funder representative on the grantee's board

A small number of philanthropies, such as the Entrepreneurs Foundation in Silicon Valley, have a foundation officer take a seat on the board of a nonprofit grantee. These funders usually take this approach because they believe that it will enable them to participate in the organization's decision making and exert authority over the nonprofit's management and governance. However, most funders avoid this approach because they think that it could further distort the power imbalance between the funder and grantee and undermine the mutual trust between these parties.[90]

Community-wide engagements

Funders—who usually have connections throughout a community—are able to have impact beyond a single nonprofit organization by playing a direct convening role. Funders can often see trends and patterns in nonprofit sector conditions. They have relationships with and are able to convene public, private, and nonprofit sector leaders to address critical community issues and provide leadership in response to changing economic, political, or social conditions.

If you are in this position, you can convene other funders, corporations, government agencies, or other groups to tackle a challenge that is of common concern. For example, funders were among the first to mobilize cities, regions, and states to respond to welfare reform, devolution, and changes resulting from managed care. Their leadership helped nonprofit organizations and communities overall develop the necessary capacity to shift how they were operating and prepare for new resource arrangements and service requirements.

Some funders focus on the overall health of the nonprofit or civil sector. For example, the Charles Stewart Mott Foundation "supports initiatives that help nonprofit groups build their internal strength so they can operate more effectively, and funds efforts to strengthen nonprofit and philanthropic membership organizations."[91]

Funders can also effectively capture the attention of other funders and increase the amount of resources available to work on a particular issue. The Ewing Marion Kauffman Foundation and Hall Family Foundation, along with fifteen other funders, have contributed over $6 million to the Kansas City Community Development Initiative to help community development corporations in Kansas and Missouri become higher-performing organizations that are better able to achieve their community redevelopment and revitalization goals. Foundations and other community leaders initiated this project to help citizens of the core city rebuild their neighborhoods physically, economically, and socially.[92]

Chapter Summary

This chapter described seven strategies you can use to build the capacity of nonprofits or communities:

Strategy 1: Program grants that promote organizational effectiveness

Strategy 2: General operating support grants

Strategy 3: Grants specifically to increase organizational effectiveness

Strategy 4: Capital financing for nonprofits and intermediaries

Strategy 5: Grant support to capacity builders and intermediaries

Strategy 6: Grants to conveners, educators, and researchers

Strategy 7: Direct management assistance

These strategies, used alone or in combination, can be a powerful support to your constituencies.

Conclusion

TODAY, NONPROFIT ORGANIZATIONS ARE BEING ASKED TO RE-spond to growing needs with limited resources. They are expected to remain steadfast in their mission and meet ever-higher standards of performance in a rapidly changing environment.

Society relies more and more on nonprofit organizations to reach shared civic goals. Their work is critical. Funders must help them acquire the tools they need to do their work well. Helping nonprofit organizations build their capacity—to develop a strong foundation to get the results they aim for—is a promising strategy available to funders.

If you haven't yet started providing capacity building support to your grant-ees, this is the time to begin. Start with small efforts to get your feet wet, open the dialogue with grantees, and begin your learning process. And then gradually, as your understanding of your constituents' needs and the range of options grows, you can add strategies.

What can funders do longer term to improve the ways that they strengthen the management and governance of nonprofit organizations? How can funders support nonprofits in their determined efforts to achieve their mission and sustain their organization? How can funders ensure that "capacity building" does not become a fad that interests funders in the short term, and then fades away as the next funder "strategy du jour" overtakes it? The following is a call to action for funders:

- **Outreach:** Strengthen and broaden the community of funders that sup-port capacity building, and make special efforts to include CEOs and trustees and government and international funders. Leaders in the field need to educate and involve a broad array of funders, encourage new voices, share experiences, demystify capacity building, and nurture the next generation of leaders in the field.

- **Research, evaluation, and dissemination:** Invest more money into research on nonprofit management and evaluation of capacity building strategies and their cost-effectiveness. Research can help develop an integrated body of knowledge and answer critical questions that inform funders' strategies. A starting point is to gather, synthesize, and disseminate the findings of existing research and develop a strategic research agenda. Increased evaluation will help document what kinds of capacity building strategies get the best results and how capacity building enhances program impact and increases nonprofit and community sustainability. Positive documented results will help attract other funders. Funders also need to share more information about failures and what did not work.

- **Funder performance:** Maintain a parallel focus on "walking the talk." If funders' own organizations are not effective, their understanding of capacity building needs will be skewed and their efforts to build the capacity of nonprofits will be severely undermined. Make sure that the values, beliefs, and practices underpinning capacity building work are institutionalized in funding organizations. Funders also need to evaluate their *own* effectiveness more and share findings about best practices with other funding organizations and the grantmaking community.

- **Delivery system:** Invest in strengthening the quality and accessibility of capacity building resources. Identify and partner with experienced, knowledgeable providers. Encourage and support the development of emerging capacity building resources who can work with increasingly diverse organizations and communities.

By helping to build the capacity of nonprofits, funders can help build organizations that will continue to meet the vital needs of society for present and future generations.

Appendices

Appendix A: International Capacity Building

Funders are increasing their support of capacity building internationally. Their goals include enhancing program impact, increasing sustainability, leveraging philanthropic dollars, building community capacity, and promoting civil society. International funders usually focus their capacity building efforts on a particular geographic area or on organizations in specific fields, such as literacy, education, economic and political development, the environment, health, or poverty.

The Open Society Institute concentrates on building the capacity of the nonprofit sector, especially in civil society organizations, in the fledgling democracies of Central and Eastern Europe. The Moriah Fund strives to enhance the effectiveness of organizations that promote women's human rights around the world. Other funders, such as the David and Lucile Packard Foundation, invest in capacity building activities that support their program grantees, which include several international nonprofits.

Challenges of international capacity building

Crossing geographic, cultural, economic, and political boundaries adds complex challenges to capacity building: different philanthropic traditions, varying roles of government, and a severe lack of resources.

Different philanthropic traditions

Outside the United States, the philanthropic and nonprofit sectors have evolved from different roots and at a different pace. Historically, tax statutes have encouraged philanthropic support in the United States. In most other countries, the legal context in which nonprofits are organized does not favor either philanthropy or support of nongovernmental organizations (NGOs).* Frequently, philanthropic activity occurs outside the formal economy, such as through cooperatives or youth clubs. In many places, particularly in Latin America, religious institutions have played the major

* Nongovernmental organizations (NGOs) are private, voluntary organizations that are not fully funded or controlled by government and that contribute to the public good on a not-for-profit basis. NGOs can be regional, national, or international and include special interest groups, development and relief agencies, environmental organizations, self-help associations, human rights organizations, public watchdog groups, labor organizations, and research and policy institutes. NGOs are the international equivalent of nonprofits in the United States.

114

philanthropic role. A funder will need to understand how to assess account-ability and transparency within vastly different contexts.

Varying roles of government

In many countries around the globe, civil society organizations are the most trusted and capable institutions, taking on responsibility as service provid-ers, social innovators, and advocates for the poor—roles that were once the purview of the state. As governments in less-developed countries face fis-cal and political uncertainty or transfer their obligations to NGOs, friction can be created between public and nonprofit sector groups. In industrial-ized countries, government roles are usually clearer and the potential for NGO–government collaboration is higher.

Undervalued local resources and the need for new resources

Funders need to value local knowledge, social networks, and expertise. Yet they also have to recognize that in many regions, there is a profound shortage of operating capital available for NGOs to strengthen their insti-tutional capacity. In the poorer countries of Africa, Asia, and Latin America, NGOs operate within environments constrained by resource deficits of all sorts—human, financial, legal, and technological. Civil unrest, the HIV/AIDS pandemic, urban violence, and environmental disasters create even more challenges for NGOs in certain areas.

How to adapt capacity building strategies

Capacity building models are not easily exported to other cultures, forcing funders to tread sensitively as they develop more responsive approaches. The basic strategies and guidelines for funders investing in capacity build-ing described in Chapters 3 and 4 apply to the international setting. Yet funders working in countries outside of the United States need to tailor their approaches, as explained below.

Be sensitive to local needs and conditions

Until recently, "experts" and funders in more affluent countries usually defined the needs of NGOs in the developing world and applied models for organizational and community capacity building without adequately taking into consideration cultural mores and dynamics. Today, NGOs are less willing to accept either the diagnosis or solutions from outside professionals. They want to set their own capacity building agenda and develop and use their own resources to do the work. International funders must understand and adapt to this request for autonomy and seek to learn from the organizations that they support.

One role for funders, and a good starting point, is facilitating the efforts of local organizations to define their own needs. The Partnership for Capacity Building in Africa is a good example. Funded by the U.S. Agency for International Development, it is working to achieve sustainable development and poverty reduction in Africa. To that end, the partnership conducts participatory organizational assessments that allow Ethiopian NGOs to understand their institutional strengths and weaknesses and define their own training and management assistance needs.[93] Other funders focus on transferring knowledge and strengthening local capacity to help local NGOs. In Hungary and Poland, the Ford Foundation and a number of other funders have provided significant support to the Rural Development and Community Foundation Initiative, which operates a train-the-trainer program to cultivate nonprofit activity and civil society.[94]

You could choose to work with knowledgeable intermediaries and local advisors who can act as a bridge between your organization and grantees. That is the path chosen by the World Bank and the Bristol-Myers Squibb Foundation in their organizational capacity building initiatives. They consulted with the Synergos Institute, an organization that is expert in developing sustainable, locally based solutions to global poverty.

Focus on enhancing financial sustainability

Many NGOs are largely dependent on international donors and operate in environments with few local philanthropic and public resources. You might want to encourage policies that promote local philanthropy and the development of civil society. But you can directly help NGOs become more financially stable by enabling them to broaden their base of support. The Rockefeller Brothers Fund, for instance, helps education-related NGOs in South Africa to diversify their income sources among individuals, companies, and government agencies.[95]

Help nongovernmental organizations develop cross-sector linkages

To succeed, NGOs usually need to develop strong ties with government agencies and corporations in their countries. You can help them develop these linkages. The Brackett Foundation, the John Merck Fund, and other funders have supported Earth Rights International, which works to enable local environmental and human rights groups to find common ground with public agencies and corporations.[96] You can also convene meetings to show the results of NGO programs or suggest to NGOs that they include people from diverse sectors on their board.

Make long-term investments in building capacity

In order to have a lasting impact, grantmakers need to make long-term investments in enhancing the effectiveness of NGOs and building community capacities internationally. Episodic, short-term support is not enough. The Ford, W. K. Kellogg, and Charles Stewart Mott foundations have all invested in building the capacity of local NGOs and civil society in South Africa for over a decade.

Appendix B: Resources

Note: Resources were selected based on their national scope and probable usefulness to funders. For information on contacting the authors or their organizations, see About the Authors, page v.

Associations, publishers, and periodicals

Alliance for Nonprofit
Management
1899 L Street, NW, 6th Floor
Washington, DC 20036
(202) 955-8406
www.allianceonline.org

The Aspen Institute
Nonprofit Sector Research Fund
One Dupont Circle, NW, Suite 700
Washington, DC 20036
(202) 736-5800 Aspen Institute
Main Number
(202) 736-5838 NSRF Information
Line
www.nonprofitresearch.org

Association for Research on
Nonprofit Organizations and
Voluntary Action (ARNOVA)
550 W. North Street, Suite 301
Indianapolis, IN 46202-3162
(317) 684-2120
www.arnova.org

BoardSource
1828 L Street, NW, Suite 900
Washington, DC 20036-5104
(202) 452-6262
www.boardsource.org

Chronicle of Philanthropy
1255 23rd Street, NW
Washington, DC 20037
www.philanthropy.com

Foundation Center
79 Fifth Avenue
New York, NY 10003
(800) 424-9836
www.fdncenter.org

Grantcraft
The Ford Foundation
320 E. 43rd Street
New York, NY 10017
(212) 573-5000
www.grantcraft.org

Grantmakers Evaluation Network
Robert Eckardt, Chair
The Cleveland Foundation
1422 Euclid Avenue, Suite 1400
Cleveland, OH 44115
(216) 861-3810
www.hogg.utexas.edu/gen

Grantmakers for Effective
Organizations (GEO)
1413 K Street NW, 2nd FL
Washington, DC 20005
(202) 898-1840
www.geofunders.org

HandsNet, Inc.
2 N. Second Street, Suite 375
San Jose, CA 95113
(408) 291-5111
www.handsnet.org

Jossey-Bass/Wiley Publications
605 Third Avenue
New York, NY 10158-6000
(212) 850-6088
www.josseybass.com

National Council of Nonprofit
Associations
1900 L Street, NW, Suite 605
Washington, DC 20036-5024
(202) 467-6262
www.ncna.org

Nonprofit and Voluntary Sector
Quarterly
University of Washington
Daniel J. Evans School of Public
Affairs
Box 353055
Seattle, WA 98195-3055
(206) 221-4629
www.evans.washington.edu/nvsq

Nonprofit Management and
Leadership Quarterly
c/o Jossey Bass/Wiley Publications
605 Third Avenue
New York, NY 10158-6000
(212) 850-6088
www.josseybass.com

Nonprofit Quarterly
18 Tremont Street, Suite 700
Boston, MA 02108
(617) 523-6565
www.nonprofitquartlerly.org

Nonprofit World
6314 Odana Road, Suite 1
Madison, WI 53719
(800) 424-7367
www.danenet.wicip.org/snpo/

Wilder Publishing Center
919 Lafond Avenue
St. Paul, MN 55104
(800) 274-6024
www.wilder.org/pubs/

Organizational assessment resources

Following is a sampling of organizational assessment resources.

Balanced Scorecard Collaborative: *The Balanced Scorecard*
Developed by Harvard Business School professor Robert Kaplan, the Balanced Scorecard is a tool that measures organizational performance related to finances, customers, internal business operations, learning and growth, and social impact.
www.bscol.com

BoardSource: *Board Self-Assessment Tool*
This full-board self-evaluation questionnaire enables board members to examine and improve board performance. The instrument is based on research related to key characteristics of effective boards.
www.boardsource.org

Community Wealth Ventures: *Capacity Screening Tool* and *Capacity Readiness Tool*
These tools help nonprofit organizations evaluate their readiness to pursue ventures to generate earned income.
www.communitywealth.com

Development Training Institute: *Leadership Self-Assessment Tool*
Competency assessment for community development organizations covering management and financial areas.
www.dtinational.org/training/tools/assess.asp

Drucker Foundation: *Self-Assessment Tool*
This participant workbook and process guide help nonprofits address four questions: Should the mission be revised? Who is the primary customer? What are our results? What does the customer value?
www.pfdf.org/leaderbooks

InnoNet: *Self-Assessment Instrument*
Offers comparative analysis of assessment tools and their use for different subject areas and groups. Field-tested.
www.innonet.org/resources

The Management Center: *Nonprofit Assessment Tool*
Eight-part, 80-item, online assessment tool intended to help organizations measure their capacity and performance in administration and leadership, board of directors, community relations and marketing, finance, human resources, planning, program, and plant and equipment.
www.tmcenter.org/

Maryland Association of Nonprofits: *Standard of Excellence*
Enables peer reviewers to measure performance for standards related to mission and program, governance, human resources, financial and legal, fundraising, and public affairs.
www.mdnonprofit.org

National Civic League: *The Civic Index*
A twelve-part self-assessment tool to help communities evaluate and improve their civic infrastructure—the interplay of people and groups through which decisions are made and problems are resolved at the community level.
www.ncl.org/publications

The Nature Conservancy: *Resources to Success*
Designed for nongovernmental organizations, this organizational assessment tool provides indicators for eight categories of nonprofit functioning. The booklet includes guidance on how to conduct an organizational self-assessment.
(800) 628-6860

Neighborhood Progress, Inc.: *Mapping the Road to Excellence: Operating Guidelines for Community Development Corporations*
Assessment tool covering legal, financial and budgeting, human resources, governance, planning, information technology, communications, and program management areas. Available in distance learning program.
www.neighborhoodprogress.org

Venture Philanthropy Partners: *Effective Capacity Building in Nonprofit Organizations*
McKinsey & Company developed the *Capacity Assessment Grid* as a self-assessment or consultant-led assessment tool, to be used in conjunction with its capacity framework.
www.venturephilanthropypartners.org/usr_doc/full_rpt.pdf
or (703) 620-8971

Wilder Center for Communities: *Organizational Assessment Guides and Measures*
Includes performance standards for community development corporations for the six components of organizational capacity referred to in this book.
(651) 642-2083

Readings on nonprofit capacity building

Backer, Thomas E. *Strengthening Nonprofits: Capacity Building and Philanthropy.* Encino, CA: Human Interaction Research Institute, 2000.

Bailey, Margo, et al. *Learning Circles Project: 15-Month Report.* Denver: Innovation Network, July 25, 2000.

_____. *Learning Circles Round I: Final Report.* Denver: Innovation Network, December 2000.

Batten, Susan T. and Peter J. York. *Evaluation of the Eureka Communities: Third Year Findings.* Bala Cynwyd, PA: Center for Assessment and Policy Development, May 1999.

Blumenthal, Barbara. "Improving the Impact of Nonprofit Consulting." *Journal for Nonprofit Management* 5 (Summer 2001): 1–17.

_____. "How Can We Help?: A Comparison of Capacity Building Programs." Unpublished paper. April 2001.

"Building Capacity: A Co-Creation Approach." *Nonprofit Quarterly* 5 (Winter 1999).

Campobasso, Laura, and Dan Davis. *Reflections on Capacity Building*. Woodland Hills, CA: California Wellness Foundation, 2001.

Center for Effective Philanthropy. *Toward a Common Language: Listening to Foundation CEOs and Other Experts Talk about Performance Measurement in Philanthropy*. Boston, MA: Center for Effective Philanthropy, 2002.

Chang, Hedy Nai-Lin, et al. *Walking the Walk: Principles for Building Community Capacity for Equity and Diversity*. Oakland, CA: California Tomorrow, Spring 2000.

Chaskin, Robert J., et al. *Building Community Capacity*. New York: Walter deGruyter, 2001.

Chieco, Kate, Deborah Koch, and Kristen Scotchmer. *Mission Possible: 200 Ways to Strengthen the Nonprofit Sector's Infrastructure*. Washington, DC: Union Institute Press, 1996.

CompassPoint Nonprofit Services and Harder & Company Community Research. *A First Map: Exploring the Market for Consulting Services to Nonprofit Organizations in the San Francisco Bay Area*. San Francisco: CompassPoint, September 2000.

Connolly, Paul. *Building to Last: A Grantmakers' Guide to Strengthening Nonprofit Organizations*. New York, NY: The Conservation Company, 2001.

Crawford, Susan. *Managing the Future: A Leader's Guide*. New York: Fund for the City of New York, July 1999.

De Vita, Carol, Cory Fleming, and Eric Twombly. *Building Capacity in Nonprofit Organizations*. Washington, DC: Urban Institute Press, 2001.

Draper, Lee. "How to 'Do' Capacity Building." *Foundation News & Commentary* 41 (September–October 2000): 32–36.

Eisenberg, Pablo. "Capacity Building: Beware the Easy Fix." *Nonprofit Quarterly* 8 (Summer 2001): 56–57.

Ewing Marion Kauffman Foundation. *Profiles in Organizational Effectiveness for Nonprofits.* Kansas City, MO: E.M. Kauffman Foundation, 2001.

Fletcher, Kathleen B. *A Study of the Long-Term Effectiveness of Technical Assistance Grants in Fundraising.* San Anselmo, CA: Unpublished paper funded by a grant from the Nonprofit Sector Research Fund of the Aspen Institute, 1992.

Glickman, Norman, and Lisa J. Servon. *By the Numbers: Measuring Community Development Corporations' Capacity.* New Brunswick, NJ: Rutgers University, 2000.

_____. "More Than Bricks and Sticks: Five Components of Community Development Corporation Capacity." *Housing Policy Debate* 9, no. 3 (1998): 497–539.

Gooding, Cheryl. "Reflections on Training as a Capacity Building Strategy." An occasional paper of the Filene Center, Tufts University, January 1996.

Grantmakers Evaluation Network and Grantmakers for Effective Organizations. *Report from GEN-GEO 2002 Conference.* "Capacity-Building for Impact: The Future of Effectiveness for Nonprofits and Foundations," Washington, DC, March 2002.

Grantmakers Evaluation Network and Grantmakers for Effective Organizations. *Report from GEN-GEO 2000 Conference.* "High-Performance Organizations: Linking Evaluation and Effectiveness." Kansas City, MO, March 2000.

Grantmakers for Effective Organizations. *Inaugural Conference Report.* Monterey, CA, October 1998.

Greene, Stephen. "Getting the Basics Right: Grantmakers Seek Effective Ways to Improve Charities' Operations." *Chronicle of Philanthropy,* 13 (May 3, 2001): 1, 9–12.

Gulati, Gita, and Kathleen Cerveny. *General Operating Support: A View from the Field: Case Studies and Reflections in Nine Grantmaking Programs.* Seattle: Grantmakers in the Arts, November 1999.

Herman, Robert D., and David O. Renz. "Theses on Nonprofit Organization Effectiveness." *Nonprofit and Voluntary Sector Quarterly* 28 (June 1999): 107–26.

Hernandez, Georgiana, and Mary G. Visher. *Creating a Culture of Inquiry: Changing Methods—and Minds—on the Use of Evaluation in Nonprofit Organizations.* San Francisco: James Irvine Foundation, 2001.

_____. *Early Lessons Learned from a Capacity Building Project Funded by the James Irvine Foundation.* San Francisco: James Irvine Foundation, March 2000.

Hruby, Laura. "Charities Urged to Focus on Management Strategies." *Chronicle of Philanthropy* 13 (September 6, 2001): 1, 9, 10, 12.

Innovation Network. *Echoes from the Field: Proven Capacity Building Principles for Nonprofits.* Washington, DC: The Environmental Support Center, December 2001.

Kibbe, Barbara, and Fred Setterberg. *Succeeding with Consultants: Self-Assessment for the Changing Nonprofit.* New York: The Foundation Center, 1992.

Lawson, R. Sam, and Sonia Barnes. *Building Philanthropic and Nonprofit Academic Centers: A View from Team Builders.* Battle Creek, MI: W.K. Kellogg Foundation, May 2001.

Lee, Janine. *Key Attributes of Effective Nonprofits: Serving Children, Youth and Families in Kansas City's Urban Core.* Kansas City, MO: E.M. Kauffman Foundation, 2000.

Letts, Christine, William Ryan, and Allen Grossman. *High Performance Nonprofit Organizations: Managing Upstream for Greater Impact.* New York: Wiley, 1998.

_____. "Virtuous Capital: What a Foundation Can Learn from Venture Capitalists." *Harvard Business Review* 75 (March–April 1997) 36–44.

Lewin Group. *Organizational Effectiveness Program Literature Review*. Los Altos, CA: David and Lucile Packard Foundation, July 2000.

Light, Paul C. *Pathways to Nonprofit Excellence*. Washington DC: Brookings Institution Press, 2002.

_____. *Making Nonprofits Work*. Washington DC: Brookings Institution Press, 2000.

_____. *Sustaining Innovation: Creating Nonprofit and Government Organizations that Innovate Naturally*. San Francisco: Jossey-Bass, 1998.

Light, Paul, and Elizabeth Hubbard. *The Capacity Building Challenge*. Washington, DC: Brookings Institution, April 2002.

Mayer, Robert N. "Capacity Building Begins at Home." *Foundation News & Commentary* 41 (September–October 2000): 48–49.

McKinsey & Company. *Effective Capacity Building in Nonprofit Organizations*. Washington, DC: Venture Philanthropy Partners, 2001.

Milton S. Eisenhower Foundation. *Lessons from the Street: Capacity Building and Replication*. Washington, DC: Milton S. Eisenhower Foundation, 2001. http://www.eisenhowerfoundation.org/frames/main_frameL.html

Mittenthal, Richard. *Effective Philanthropy: The Importance of Focus*. New York: The Conservation Company, 1999.

Nye, Nancy, and Norman Glickman. "Working Together: Building Capacity for Community Development." *Housing Policy Debate* 11, no. 1 (2000): 163–198.

Nye, Nancy. *Sustainable Strength: An Interim Report of the Capacity Building Program Evaluation*. New York: Corporation for Supportive Housing, December 1998.

Oster, Sharon. *Strategic Management for Nonprofit Organizations: Theory and Cases*. New York: Oxford University Press, 1995.

Philbin, Ann. *Capacity Building Work with Social Justice Organizations: Views from the Field*. New York: Ford Foundation, 1998.

Philbin, Ann, and Sandra Mikush. *A Framework for Organizational Development: The Why, What and How of OD Work.* Winston-Salem, NC: Mary Reynolds Babcock Foundation, 2000. www.mrbf.org

Porter, Michael E., and Mark K. Kramer. "Philanthropy's New Agenda: Creating Value." *Harvard Business Review* 77 (November–December 1999): 121–130.

Prager, Denis J. Raising the Value of Philanthropy. Washington, DC: Grantmakers in Health, January 1999.

Proscio, Tony. *In Other Words: A Plea for Plain Speaking in Foundations.* New York: Edna McConnell Clark Foundation, 2000.

Rodriguez, Aida, and Joseph Pereira. "The Roles of Intermediaries in Organizational Capacity Building." Paper presented at the Association for Public Policy Analysis and Management, 2000 Annual Research Conference, October 31, 2000.

Ryan, William. *Nonprofit Capital: A Review of Problems and Strategies.* New York and Washington, DC: Rockefeller Foundation and Fannie Mae Foundation, 2001.

Sawhill, John C., and David Williamson. "Mission Impossible? Measuring Success in Nonprofit Organizations." *Nonprofit Management & Leadership* 11 (2000): 371–386.

Seltzer, Michael, Judith Simpson, and Rikki Abzug. *Promoting Organizational Learning and Excellence among Cleveland's Nonprofit Organizations.* New York: Robert J. Milano Graduate School of Management and Urban Policy, New School University, 2000.

Seltzer, Michael, and Joseph Stillman. *Strengthening New York City Nonprofit Organizations: A Blueprint for Action.* New York: United Way of New York City and New York Community Trust (prepared by The Conservation Company, 1993).

The Stevens Group. *Illinois Nonprofits: Building Capacity for the Next Century.* Chicago: Illinois Facilities Fund and Donors Forum of Chicago, 1998.

Thomas, Jim. *Evaluation Report: The Initiative on Effective Use of Consultants.* Los Altos, CA: David and Lucile Packard Foundation, January 1999.

Tuan, Melinda. "Social Purpose Enterprises and Venture Philanthropy in the New Millenium." In *Investor Perspectives*, Vol. 2. San Francisco: The Roberts Enterprise Development Fund, 1999.

Wahl, Ellen, Michele Cahill, and Norman Fruchter. *Building Capacity: A Review of Technical Assistance Strategies.* New York: Institute for Education and Social Policy, New York University, 1998.

Walker, Christopher, and Mark Weinheimer. *Community Development in the 1990s.* Washington, DC: Urban Institute Press, 1998.

Weinheimer & Associates. *Building the Capacity of Indianapolis' CDCs: Lessons from Assessing 13 CDCs.* Washington, DC: Indianapolis Neighborhood Partnership, 1997.

Appendix C: Worksheets

Worksheets are also available online to purchasers of this book. To use the online worksheets, visit the following web address:

http://www.wilder.org/pubs/workshts/pubs_worksheets1.html?377shp

DESIGN YOUR PLANNING PROCESS

Instructions: Use questions 1–3 to outline your planning process, determine its duration and the amount of time required, and describe who will be involved. Fill in the chart for question 4 to start developing your plan.

1. Describe your general approach and pace for the planning process:

- How do you intend to tailor the process to your organization's specific circumstances?
- How much time do you want to devote to the planning process?
- What is your estimate for how long the planning process will last?

2. Describe who will be involved in the planning process:

- Will you use a planning committee?
- Who will be on it?
- Who will lead it?
- What other people do you want to involve in the planning process?

3. Do you need outside help? What kind of help?

4. Using the chart on the following page, set a timeline for your process and identify participants for each step. As you read through each step in the planning process, add details about the specific tasks you will use to complete the step.

Step	Key Participants	Start Date	End Date	Financial Requirements
1. Plan to Plan Task One: Establish a general approach and pace Task Two: Determine who will be involved Task Three: Decide whether you need outside help Task Four: Create a timeline for your planning process				
2. Take Stock Task One: Determine your organization's readiness and capabilities Task Two: Review external needs and resources Task Three: Acknowledge your organization's values and assumptions				
3. Set Direction Task One: Define your goals and objectives Task Two: Select strategies Task Three: Commit resources				
4. Take Action and Evaluate Task One: Implement strategies Task Two: Evaluate your efforts				

DETERMINE YOUR ORGANIZATION'S READINESS AND CAPABILITIES

Instructions: Use this worksheet to summarize your organizational assessment.

1. Commitment: Do key decision makers in our organization support strengthening nonprofit capacity and infrastructure? Do staff, trustees, and donors understand what capacity building is? Do they support a capacity building effort at this time?

☐ In Good Shape   ☐ Needs Work

2. Leadership: Do we have the leadership and staff expertise to undertake this effort?

☐ In Good Shape   ☐ Needs Work

3. Practices: Do we place a high value on our own organizational effectiveness? What are our strengths as an organization? What aspects of our organization need to be strengthened?

Use the following chart to note your assessment of current practices in your organization.

Current Practice	In Good Shape	Needs Attention Sometime	Needs Work Before Proceeding
1. Our current grantmaking practices encourage grantees to build strong organizations.			
2. Our mission is clear, understood, and aligned with current programs.			
3. Our mission can be interpreted to include capacity building.			
4. We have a current strategic plan that we use and monitor.			
5. We regularly obtain and use input from our constituencies in making programming decisions.			
6. Our board is clear about its roles and responsibilities.			
7. Our board functions well as a governing body.			
8. Our board and staff are representative of the diversity of the communities we serve.			
9. We collaborate appropriately with other organizations.			
10. We systematically evaluate the impact of our grantmaking and use findings to improve our funding practices.			

4. Financial Resources: What level of investment are we willing to make for capacity building and for what time period?

☐ In Good Shape   ☐ Needs Work

5. Organizational Assets: What nonmonetary assets or organizational capabilities do we possess that could benefit the community?

☐ In Good Shape   ☐ Needs Work

6. Reputation: Do we have the necessary regard and trust of the community to launch a capacity building effort?

☐ In Good Shape   ☐ Needs Work

7. Conclusions: How can we improve our own practices before we launch our capacity building work?

☐ In Good Shape   ☐ Needs Work

Note especially any areas that you checked as "needing work."

REVIEW EXTERNAL NEEDS AND RESOURCES

Instructions: On this worksheet, record what you learned regarding capacity building needs and resources.

Nonprofit and Community Needs

1. What organizations or groups will we target for capacity building support?

2. What are the strengths or assets of these organizations?

3. What trends or challenges are they facing?

4. What kind of support do they need?

　a. What kind of assistance would help them become more effective and have greater impact?

　b. Are there patterns in needs or clusters of organizations that have similar needs?

Community Resources

5. What are other funders doing? Are there gaps in assistance?

6. What capacity building resources exist in the community? What are their strengths and weaknesses? Are there significant gaps?

7. What promising capacity building approaches should we consider exploring?

ACKNOWLEDGE YOUR VALUES AND ASSUMPTIONS

Instructions: In the chart below, record your organization's values in column one. In column two, record the implications of these values for your goals, strategy, or financial allocations. Review the values you've identified with key decision makers in your organization. Note the confirmed values that will guide your capacity building plans.

Values	Implications for capacity building goals, strategy or approach, and allocation of resources
Values related to organizational ends:	
Values related to the kind of capacity you want to build:	
Values related to program imperatives or constraints:	
Values related to whom you will serve:	
Values related to your role with grantees and the community:	

DEFINE YOUR GOALS AND OBJECTIVES

Instructions: Have your planning committee answer the following questions.

1. List the major goals of your capacity building activities. Explain how each goal helps address needs and is feasible. Describe the types and number of nonprofit organizations that you are trying to influence and where they are located.

2. For each goal, list one or two specific objectives. Make sure that they are based on your goals and incorporate time frames and measurable results so that you can document and monitor your progress.

3. Describe how you will measure success during and after strategy implementation.

   Published by the Amherst H. Wilder Foundation · Copyright ©2002

ASSESS STRATEGY OPTIONS

Instructions:

- *Use this worksheet to assess each of your strategy options. (Make copies of this worksheet for each alternative being considered.) Describe the strategy, and then assess it according to the criteria in the chart below. Add other criteria that are important to you, such as the level of risk or innovation, the flexibility, or the cost-effectiveness of the strategy.*

- *For each criterion, assign a score on a scale from 1 to 10 (with "1" meaning that the strategy option does not meet the criterion well and "10" meaning that the strategy meets the criterion very well). Write the total score at the bottom of the chart.*

- *After assessing each option, compare your results and select the highest-ranking options.*

Strategy description:

Criteria	Score (1–10)
• Helps you achieve stated goals and objectives	
• Is congruent with your organization's mission, values, and culture	
• Addresses a perceived need in the community	
• Coordinates with other programs	
• Is feasible, fits your organization's readiness and capability, and takes advantage of your organization's competitive advantages and distinctive competencies	
• Responds to external needs and resources	
• Has adequate funding and human resources devoted to it	
• Is acceptable to decision makers and other stakeholders	
• Other criteria (list):	
TOTAL	

Overall comment on attractiveness of this strategy:

SELECT STRATEGIES

Instructions: *Use this worksheet if you plan to provide support to capacity builders, researchers, educators, or conveners, or if you plan to provide direct management assistance. Check off the means of assistance you plan to support or employ.*

Organizational area to which the activity is related	Means of Providing Assistance						
	Referrals	Research	Publica-tions	Education and Training	Peer Exchanges	Convening	Consulting
Mission, Vision, and Strategy							
Strategic planning							
Scenario planning							
Organizational assessment							
Organizational development							
Governance and Leadership							
Leadership development							
Board development							
Executive transition							
Program Delivery and Impact							
Program design and development							
Evaluation							
Strategic Relationships							
Collaboration and strategic restructuring							
Marketing and communications							

Organizational area to which the activity is related	Means of Providing Assistance						
	Referrals	Research	Publica-tions	Education and Training	Peer Exchanges	Convening	Consulting
Resource Development							
Fund development							
Business planning for revenue-generating activities							
Internal Operations							
Human resource management and training							
Financial management							
Operations							
Technology and information systems							
Facility planning							
Legal issues							
Volunteer recruitment and management							
Conflict resolution							

COMMIT RESOURCES

Instructions: Use this worksheet throughout your planning to calculate budget requirements for your capacity building plan. Note that this list may not include all operating costs for your organization. List direct and indirect costs associated with the strategies you have selected.

Budget Item	Year 1	Year 2	Year 3

Salaries and benefits
    Staff: _____ Full-time employees
    Salaries
    Benefits			

Grant payout
    Number of grants
    Average size of grants			

Independent contractors
    Planning consultant
    Capacity building providers
    Evaluation
    Communications/web site
    Internal organizational consulting			

Copying/printing
    Guidelines
    Brochures
    Program materials			

Space			

Budget Item	Year 1	Year 2	Year 3
Memberships			

Travel
  Transportation
  Room and board			

Conference costs			

Meeting costs
  Space rental
  Meals/refreshments			

Publications, subscriptions			
Memberships			
Equipment purchase and maintenance			
TOTAL			

IMPLEMENT STRATEGIES

Instructions: Use this worksheet to plan the implementation of your strategies. For each strategy, answer the questions below. Make a copy of this worksheet for each strategy. Involve those who will implement the strategies in filling out this worksheet.

1. What strategy will you pursue?

2. How does this strategy help you achieve your goals and objectives, address needs, and build on your capabilities?

3. What specific steps do you need to take to put this strategy to work? Who is responsible for each task? When will each task start and end? Who needs to be kept informed of progress made on the task?

4. What financial and skill resources, internally, will your foundation apply to put this strategy in place?

5. How much are you prepared to allocate each year via grants for this strategy?

6. How long will you commit to carrying out this strategy?

7. What are potential obstacles to implementing this strategy and how do you intend to overcome them?

CREATE AN EVALUATION DESIGN

Instructions: Use this worksheet with your evaluator to articulate your evaluation questions, success indicators, required information, and data collection methods.

Evaluation Questions	Indicators	Information Required	Data Collection Methods
What critical questions do you want to answer?	*What will indicate success for the evaluation questions?*	*What is the source of the information you need?*	*What tools will you use to collect the information you need?*
Question 1:			
Question 2:			
Question 3:			
Question 4:			

 Published by the Amherst H. Wilder Foundation · Copyright ©2002

CREATE A PROGRAM EVALUATION LOGIC MODEL

Instructions: *Begin by filling in the goals and objectives for your funded activity. Then identify the program's inputs, activities, outputs, and outcomes. Use this worksheet with the evaluator to create a logic model for your program.*

Inputs What resources do you need for the activity?	Activities What will happen during the funding period?	Outputs What will the activities produce immediately?	Outcomes How will clients or constituents be different as a result of the activity?

Notes

[1] Barbara Kibbe, interview conducted by the Conservation Company for *Building to Last: A Grantmaker's Guide for Strengthening Nonprofit Organizations* (New York: Conservation Company, 2001).

[2] McKinsey & Company. *Effective Capacity Building in Nonprofit Organizations.* (Washington, DC: Venture Philanthropy Partners, 2001), 29.

[3] Frazieta Klasen, interview conducted by The Conservation Company for *Building to Last: A Grantmaker's Guide for Strengthening Nonprofit Organizations* (New York: Conservation Company, 2001).

[4] Ann Philbin, *Capacity Building Work with Social Justice Organizations: Views from the Field*, (New York: Ford Foundation, 1998), 5.

[5] Carol De Vita, Cory Fleming, and Eric Twombly, *Building Capacity in Nonprofit Organizations*, (Washington, DC: Urban Institute Press, 2001). This figure was inspired by the framework presented on pp. 4–5 of the Winter 1999 "Capacity Building" issue of *Nonprofit Quarterly*.

[6] Michael E. Porter, and Mark R. Kramer. "Philanthropy's New Agenda: Creating Value," *Harvard Business Review* 77 (November–December 1999): 123–124.

[7] Grantmakers Evaluation Network and Grantmakers for Effective Organizations, "High Performance Organizations: Linking Evaluation and Effectiveness," *Report from 2000 GEN-GEO Conference* (Kansas City, MO: March 2000), 2.

[8] Adapted from Paul Fate and Linda Hoskins, *Organizational Assessment Guides and Measures* (St. Paul, MN: Wilder Center for Communities, 2001). Some of these components are derived from Norman J. Glickman and Lisa J. Servon, "More Than Bricks and Sticks: Five Components of Community Development Corporation Capacity," *Housing Policy Debate* 9, no. 3 (1998): 497–539.

[9] Christine W. Letts, William P. Ryan, and Allen Grossman, *High Performance Nonprofit Organizations: Managing Upstream for Greater Impact* (New York: Wiley, 1998).

10 Joseph A. Connor, Stephanie Kadel-Taras, and Diane Vinokur-Kaplan, "The Role of Nonprofit Management Support Organizations in Sustaining Community Collaborations," *Nonprofit Management & Leadership* 10 (Winter 1999): 127–136.

11 Thomas E. Backer, *Strengthening Nonprofits: Capacity Building and Philanthropy* (Northridge, CA: Human Interaction Research Institute, March 2000), 3–4.

12 Susan Kenny Stevens and Diane Espaldon, *Investing in Capacity: How the Working Capital Fund Promotes Sustainable Change* (New York: Ford Foundation, 2001), 58–59.

13 During a presentation at the December 1999 Alliance for Nonprofit Management conference in Boston, Jim Abernathy of the Environmental Support Center described the "ménage à trois" relationships that funders, nonprofits, and capacity builders often have.

14 Jan Masaoka's keynote speech to the Alliance for Nonprofit Management at its April 2001 conference in Cleveland.

15 Susan Crawford, *Managing the Future: A Leader's Guide* (New York: Fund for the City of New York, July 1999), 27.

16 Mary G. Visher and Georgiana Hernandez, *Early Lessons Learned from a Capacity Building Project Funded by the James Irvine Foundation* (San Francisco: James Irvine Foundation, March 2000), 13.

17 Milton S. Eisenhower Foundation, *Lessons from the Street: Capacity Building and Replication* (Washington, DC: Milton S. Eisenhower Foundation, 2001), 44.

18 *Report from 2000 GEN-GEO Conference*, 2.

19 Fazzi Associates, "Organizational Effectiveness Grantmaking Program," in *May 21, 1999, Report for the Irene E. and George A. Davis Foundation* (Springfield, MA: Irene E. and George A. Davis Foundation, 1999), 1.

20 www.ge.com/community/news/2001/feb/management.html.

21 Michael Seltzer and Joseph Stillman, *Strengthening New York City Nonprofit Organizations: A Blueprint for Action* (New York: United Way of New York City and New York Community Trust, 1993), 3.

22 Conservation Company, *Needs Assessment of Community-Based Organizations Serving Persons Affected by HIV/AIDS in New York City* (New York: HIV Health and Human Services Planning Council of New York, September 2001), 2.

23 Michael Seltzer, Judith Simpson, and Rikki Abzug, *Promoting Organizational Learning and Excellence among Cleveland's Nonprofit Organizations* (New York: Robert J. Milano Graduate School of Management and Urban Policy, New School University, 2000), 35–36.

24 www.headwatersfund.org/about.html

25 www.techrocks.org

26 www.nesst.org

27 Nancy Nye, *Sustainable Strength: An Interim Report of the Capacity Building Program Evaluation* (New York: Corporation for Supportive Housing, December 1998), i.

28 Community Partners, "Youth Development Resource Project Fact Sheet" prepared for a June 14, 1996, meeting organized by the Southern California Association for Philanthropy on the topic of technical assistance for youth-serving organizations.

29 www.nif.org

30 Venture Philanthropy Partners, *Venture Philanthropy 2002: Advancing Nonprofit Performance Through High-Engagement Grantmaking* (Washington, DC: Venture Philanthropy Partners, 2002), 94.

31 Correspondence between Gayle Williams of Mary Reynolds Babcock Foundation and Paul Connolly, April 2002.

32 "Guidelines for Technical Assistance Small Grants Program" (New York: New York Foundation, November 2000).

33 "Nonprofit Management Fund fact sheet" (Milwaukee: Greater Milwaukee Foundation, January 2000).

34 "The Eugene and Agnes E. Meyer Foundation Nonprofit Sector Advancement Fund fact sheet" (Washington, DC: Eugene and Agnes E. Meyer Foundation, January 2000).

35 "Enhancing the Effectiveness of Grantees Guidelines," www.packfound. org

36 Melinda Tuan, "Social Purpose Enterprises and Venture Philanthropy in the New Millennium," in *Investor Perspectives,* vol. 2 (San Francisco: Roberts Enterprise Development Fund, 1999), 19.

37 Stephen Greene, "Getting the Basics Right: Grantmakers Seek Effective Ways to Improve Charities' Operations," *Chronicle of Philanthropy* 13 (May 3, 2001): 10.

38 "Is Core Operating Support Strategic Philanthropy?" 2001 Council on Foundations conference presentation by Michael Bailin, President of Edna McConnell Clark Foundation, (Philadelphia: May 2, 2001).

39 "Hartford Foundation for Public Giving Request for Proposal, Multi-Service Agencies Initiative," (Hartford: Hartford Foundation for Public Giving, January 2000).

40 Handouts from the presentation "Good Governance Makes for Good Grants (and Sense) for the Grant Seeker and the Grant Maker," by David Odahowski, President of the Edyth Bush Charitable Foundation, at the National Center for Nonprofit Boards 1999 National Leadership Forum, November 16, 1999, Washington, DC.

41 Gita Gulati and Kathleen Cerveny. *General Operating Support: A View From the Field,* (Seattle: Grantmakers in the Arts, November 1999): 12.

42 Nye, Nancy, *Sustainable Strength,* i.

43 Community Partners, "Youth Development Resource Project Fact Sheet."

44 Gulati and Cerveny, *General Operating Support,* 54.

45 "The Eugene and Agnes E. Meyer Foundation Nonprofit Sector Advancement Fund 2002 Management Assistance Program Guidelines and Grantee Reporting and Self-Evaluation Form."

[46] This chart was inspired by one developed by Pamela Leland, Laura Otten, and Karen Simmons for a session they conducted entitled "Assessing Your Management Support Organization" on April 20, 2001 at the Alliance for Nonprofit Management conference in Cleveland.

[47] Nye, *Sustainable Strength,* ii.

[48] Gulati and Cerveny, *General Operating Support,* 12.

[49] Greene, "Getting the Basics Right," 11.

[50] Odahowski, "Good Governance Makes for Good Grants."

[51] "Guidelines for Leadership and Enhanced Assistance Program" (Washington, DC: Environmental Support Center, December 1999).

[52] Michael Seltzer and Michael Cunningham, "General Operating Support vs. Project Support, a 75-Year-Old Debate Revisited" (Unpublished paper, January 1990).

[53] Denis J. Prager, *Raising the Value of Philanthropy,* (Washington, DC: Grantmakers in Health, January 1999), 18.

[54] Paul Light, *Sustaining Innovation: Creating Nonprofit and Government Organizations That Innovate Naturally,* (San Francisco: Jossey-Bass, Inc., 1998).

[55] Gulati and Cerveny, *General Operating Support,* 54.

[56] www.liscnet.org/twincities/programs

[57] Grant Guidelines, Broward County Cultural Grants 2002–2003.

[58] www.mrbf.org/grantmaking

[59] www.surdna.org/programs/organization

[60] www.hfpg.org

[61] www.fdncenter.org/grantmaker/Bremer

[62] www.scap.org/laufindex.htm

[63] www.tbf.org.

[64] Greene, "Getting the Basics Right," 10.

65 Cornerstone Consulting Group, *Communities in the Balance: Reflections on the Neighborhood Preservation Initiative Final Report* (Houston: Cornerstone Consulting Group, 1998).

66 Ellen Schall, *Building Capacity of Non-Profits: Lessons from the Field* (Unpublished paper, New York: New York University Wagner School of Public Service, 2000), 11.

67 *St. Paul Foundation Annual Report* (St. Paul: St. Paul Foundation, 2001).

68 Illinois Facilities Fund and Donors Forum of Chicago, *Illinois Nonprofits: Building Capacity for the Next Century* (Chicago: Illinois Facilities Fund and Donors Forum of Chicago, 1998), 2.

69 William Ryan, *Nonprofit Capital: A Review of Problems and Strategies* (New York and Washington, DC: Rockefeller Foundation and Fannie Mae Foundation, 2001), 7.

70 www.cccif.org

71 Ryan, *Nonprofit Capital,* 8.

72 Ibid., 9.

73 www.workingcapitalfund.org

74 Hartford Foundation for Public Giving, "Components of Nonprofit Management Program Fact Sheet," (March 2000); Eugene and Agnes E. Meyer Foundation, "Nonprofit Sector Advancement Fund Fact Sheet" (March 2000).

75 www.tigerfoundation.org/jtpage.html

76 May 30, 2000, Ford Foundation press release "Ford Foundation's $42.5 million initiative to benefit 28 arts organizations across the country."

77 Audrey Newman, *Built to Change: Catalytic Capacity Building in Nonprofit Organizations* (Los Altos, CA: David and Lucile Packard Foundation, April 2001), 10.

78 www.cnm.org/events/awards/frist.htm

79 www.nonprofitresearch.org/information1524/information.htm

80 Barbara Kibbe, interview conducted by the Conservation Company for *Building to Last: A Grantmaker's Guide for Strengthening Nonprofit Organizations* (New York: Conservation Company, 2001).

81 www.fordfound.org.

82 Lewin Group, *Organizational Effectiveness Program Literature Review* (Los Altos, CA: David and Lucile Packard Foundation, July 2000), 10.

83 R. Sam Lawson and Sonia Barnes, *Building Philanthropic and Nonprofit Academic Centers: A View from Team Builders* (Battle Creek, MI: W. K. Kellogg Foundation, May 2001), 18–19.

84 Darlene Siska, "Strengthening Philanthropy." *Foundation News & Commentary* 41 (May/June 2000): 7–8.

85 LISC New York City, "Laying Strong Foundations," *Neighborhood Notes* (Summer 2000): 3.

86 Tania Dorowolski, "Learning Communities: The Wave of the Future," *Nonprofit Quarterly* 6 (Winter 1999): 30–37.

87 Tuan, "Social Purpose Enterprises," 9.

88 Correspondence between Marc Breslaw of New Israel Fund and Wilder Foundation, August 2002.

89 Paul Shoemaker, "Adventures in Philanthropy: What Works and What Doesn't," *Responsive Philanthropy* need vol. (Spring 2001): 6–9.

90 Thomas J. Bilitteri, "Venturing a Bet on Giving," *Chronicle of Philanthropy* 12 (June 1, 2000): 1, 7–12.

91 http://www.mott.org/programs/cs-us.asp

92 www.emkf.org

93 www.worldbank.org/html/extr/extme/2200.html

94 Ann Philbin and Tim Cross. "The Role of Leadership in Promoting Capacity Building Efforts" *The Nonprofit Quarterly*, 6 (Winter 1999): 43.

95 www.rbf.org/saprogram.html

96 www.earthrights.org

Index

Notes

More results-oriented books from the Amherst H. Wilder Foundation

Collaboration

Collaboration Handbook
Creating, Sustaining, and Enjoying the Journey
by Michael Winer and Karen Ray

Shows you how to get a collaboration going, set goals, determine everyone's roles, create an action plan, and evaluate the results. Includes a case study of one collaboration from start to finish, helpful tips on how to avoid pitfalls, and worksheets to keep everyone on track.

192 pages, softcover   Item # 069032

Collaboration: What Makes It Work, 2nd Ed.
by Paul Mattessich, PhD, Marta Murray-Close, BA, and Barbara Monsey, MPH

An in-depth review of current collaboration research. Major findings are summarized, critical conclusions are drawn, and twenty key factors influencing successful collaborations are identified. Includes The Wilder Collaboration Factors Inventory, which groups can use to assess their collaboration.

104 pages, softcover   Item # 069326

The Nimble Collaboration
Fine-Tuning Your Collaboration for Lasting Success
by Karen Ray

Shows you ways to make your existing collaboration more responsive, flexible, and productive. Provides three key strategies to help your collaboration respond quickly to changing environments and participants.

136 pages, softcover   Item # 069288

Funder's Guides

Community Visions, Community Solutions
Grantmaking for Comprehensive Impact
by Joseph A. Connor and Stephanie Kadel-Taras

Helps foundations, community funds, government agencies, and other grantmakers uncover a community's highest aspiration for itself, and support and sustain strategic efforts to get to workable solutions.

128 pages, softcover   Item # 06930X

Strengthening Nonprofit Performance
A Funder's Guide to Capacity Building
Paul Connolly and Carol Lukas

This practical guide synthesizes the most recent capacity building practice and research into a collection of strategies, steps, and examples that you can use to get started on or improve funding to strengthen nonprofit organizations.

176 pages, softcover   Item # 069377

Management & Planning

The Best of the Board Café
Hands-on Solutions for Nonprofit Boards
by Jan Masaoka, CompassPoint Nonprofit Services

Gathers the most requested articles from the e-newsletter, *Board Café*. You'll find a lively menu of ideas, information, opinions, news, and resources to help board members give and get the most out of their board service.

232 pages, softcover   Item # 069407

Bookkeeping Basics
What Every Nonprofit Bookkeeper Needs to Know
by Debra L. Ruegg and Lisa M. Venkatrathnam

Complete with step-by-step instructions, a glossary of accounting terms, detailed examples, and handy reproducible forms, this book will enable you to successfully meet the basic bookkeeping requirements of your nonprofit organization—even if you have little or no formal accounting training.

128 pages, softcover   Item # 069296

Consulting with Nonprofits: A Practitioner's Guide
by Carol A. Lukas

A step-by-step, comprehensive guide for consultants. Addresses the art of consulting, how to run your business, and much more. Also includes tips and anecdotes from thirty skilled consultants.

240 pages, softcover   Item # 069172

For current prices, a catalog, or to order call 800-274-6024

The Wilder Nonprofit Field Guide to
Crafting Effective Mission and Vision Statements
by Emil Angelica

Guides you through two six-step processes that result in a mission statement, vision statement, or both. Shows how a clarified mission and vision lead to more effective leadership, decisions, fundraising, and management. Includes tips, sample statements, and worksheets.

88 pages, softcover   Item # 06927X

The Wilder Nonprofit Field Guide to
Developing Effective Teams
by Beth Gilbertsen and Vijit Ramchandani

Helps you understand, start, and maintain a team. Provides tools and techniques for writing a mission statement, setting goals, conducting effective meetings, creating ground rules to manage team dynamics, making decisions in teams, creating project plans, and developing team spirit.

80 pages, softcover   Item # 069202

The Five Life Stages of Nonprofit Organizations
Where You Are, Where You're Going, and What to Expect When You Get There
by Judith Sharken Simon with J. Terence Donovan

Shows you what's "normal" for each development stage which helps you plan for transitions, stay on track, and avoid unnecessary struggles. Includes The Wilder Nonprofit Life Stage Assessment to plot your organization's progress in seven arenas of organization development.

128 pages, softcover   Item # 069229

The Lobbying and Advocacy Handbook for Nonprofit Organizations
Shaping Public Policy at the State and Local Level
by Marcia Avner

The Lobbying and Advocacy Handbook is a planning guide and resource for nonprofit organizations that want to influence issues that matter to them. This book will help you decide whether to lobby and then put plans in place to make it work.

240 pages, softcover   Item # 069261

The Manager's Guide to Program Evaluation:
Planning, Contracting, and Managing for Useful Results
by Paul W. Mattessich, Ph.D.

Explains how to plan and manage an evaluation that will help identify your organization's successes, share information with key audiences, and improve services.

96 pages, softcover   Item # 069385

The Nonprofit Board Member's Guide to Lobbying and Advocacy
by Marcia Avner

Written specifically for board members, this guide helps organizations increase their impact on policy decisions. It reveals how board members can be involved in planning for and implementing successful lobbying efforts.

96 pages, softcover   Item # 069393

The Nonprofit Mergers Workbook
The Leader's Guide to Considering, Negotiating, and Executing a Merger
by David La Piana

A merger can be a daunting and complex process. Save time, money, and untold frustration with this highly practical guide that makes the process manageable and controllable. Includes case studies, decision trees, twenty-two worksheets, checklists, tips, and complete step-by-step guidance from seeking partners to writing the merger agreement, and more.

240 pages, softcover   Item # 069210

The Nonprofit Mergers Workbook Part II
Unifying the Organization after a Merger
by La Piana Associates

Once the merger agreement is signed, the question becomes: How do we make this merger work? *Part II* helps you create a comprehensive plan to achieve *integration*—bringing together people, programs, processes, and systems from two (or more) organizations into a single, unified whole.

248 pages, includes CD-ROM   Item # 069415

Resolving Conflict in Nonprofit Organizations
The Leader's Guide to Finding Constructive Solutions
by Marion Peters Angelica

Helps you identify conflict, decide whether to intervene, uncover and deal with the true issues, and design and conduct a conflict resolution process. Includes exercises to learn and practice conflict resolution skills, guidance on handling unique conflicts such as harassment and discrimination, and when (and where) to seek outside help with litigation, arbitration, and mediation.

192 pages, softcover   Item # 069164

For current prices or to order visit us online at ⌨ www.wilder.org/pubs

Strategic Planning Workbook for Nonprofit Organizations, Revised and Updated
by Bryan Barry

Chart a wise course for your nonprofit's future. This time-tested workbook gives you practical step-by-step guidance, real-life examples, one nonprofit's complete strategic plan, and easy-to-use worksheets.

144 pages, softcover   Item # 069075

Marketing & Fundraising

The Wilder Nonprofit Field Guide to
Conducting Successful Focus Groups
by Judith Sharken Simon

Shows how to collect valuable information without a lot of money or special expertise. Using this proven technique, you'll get essential opinions and feedback to help you check out your assumptions, do better strategic planning, improve services or products, and more.

80 pages, softcover   Item # 069199

Coping with Cutbacks:
The Nonprofit Guide to Success When Times Are Tight
by Emil Angelica and Vincent Hyman

Shows you practical ways to involve business, government, and other nonprofits to solve problems together. Also includes 185 cutback strategies you can put to use right away.

128 pages, softcover   Item # 069091

The Wilder Nonprofit Field Guide to
Fundraising on the Internet
by Gary M. Grobman, Gary B. Grant, and Steve Roller

Your quick road map to using the Internet for fundraising. Shows you how to attract new donors, troll for grants, get listed on sites that assist donors, and learn more about the art of fundraising. Includes detailed reviews of 77 web sites useful to fundraisers, including foundations, charities, prospect research sites, and sites that assist donors.

64 pages, softcover   Item # 069180

Marketing Workbook for Nonprofit Organizations Volume I: Develop the Plan
by Gary J. Stern

Don't just wish for results—get them! Here's how to create a straightforward, usable marketing plan. Includes the six Ps of Marketing, how to use them effectively, a sample marketing plan, tips on using the Internet, and worksheets.

208 pages, softcover   Item # 069253

Marketing Workbook for Nonprofit Organizations Volume II: Mobilize People for Marketing Success
by Gary J. Stern

Put together a successful promotional campaign based on the most persuasive tool of all: personal contact. Learn how to mobilize your entire organization, its staff, volunteers, and supporters in a focused, one-to-one marketing campaign. Comes with *Pocket Guide for Marketing Representatives.* In it, your marketing representatives can record key campaign messages and find motivational reminders.

192 pages, softcover   Item # 069105

Venture Forth! The Essential Guide to Starting a Moneymaking Business in Your Nonprofit Organization
by Rolfe Larson

The most complete guide on nonprofit business development. Building on the experience of dozens of organizations, this handbook gives you a time-tested approach for finding, testing, and launching a successful nonprofit business venture.

272 pages, softcover   Item # 069245

Vital Communities

Community Building: What Makes It Work
by Wilder Research Center

Reveals twenty-eight keys to help you build community more effectively. Includes detailed descriptions of each factor, case examples of how they play out, and practical questions to assess your work.

112 pages, softcover   Item # 069121

Community Economic Development Handbook
by Mihailo Temali

A concrete, practical handbook to turning any neighborhood around. It explains how to start a community economic development organization, and then lays out the steps of four proven and powerful strategies for revitalizing inner-city neighborhoods.

288 pages, softcover   Item # 069369

The Wilder Nonprofit Field Guide to
Conducting Community Forums
by Carol Lukas and Linda Hoskins

Provides step-by-step instruction to plan and carry out exciting, successful community forums that will educate the public, build consensus, focus action, or influence policy.

128 pages, softcover   Item # 069318

Violence Prevention & Intervention

The Little Book of Peace
Designed and illustrated by Kelly O. Finnerty

A pocket-size guide to help people think about violence and talk about it with their families and friends. You may download a free copy of *The Little Book of Peace* from our web site at www.wilder.org.

24 pages (minimum order 10 copies)   Item # 069083
*Also available in **Spanish** and **Hmong** language editions.*

Journey Beyond Abuse: A Step-by-Step Guide to Facilitating Women's Domestic Abuse Groups
*by Kay-Laurel Fischer, MA, LP,
and Michael F. McGrane, LICSW*

Create a program where women increase their understanding of the dynamics of abuse, feel less alone and isolated, and have a greater awareness of channels to safety. This book includes twenty-one group activities that you can combine to create groups of differing length and focus.

208 pages, softcover   Item # 069148

Moving Beyond Abuse: Stories and Questions for Women Who Have Lived with Abuse
(Companion guided journal to *Journey Beyond Abuse*)

A series of stories and questions that can be used in coordination with the sessions provided in the facilitator's guide or with the guidance of a counselor in other forms of support.

88 pages, softcover   Item # 069156

Foundations for Violence-Free Living:
A Step-by-Step Guide to Facilitating Men's
Domestic Abuse Groups
by David J. Mathews, MA, LICSW

A complete guide to facilitating a men's domestic abuse program. Includes twenty-nine activities, detailed guidelines for presenting each activity, and a discussion of psychological issues that may arise out of each activity.

240 pages, softcover   Item # 069059

On the Level
(Participant's workbook to *Foundations for
Violence-Free Living*)

Contains forty-nine worksheets including midterm and final evaluations. Men can record their progress.

160 pages, softcover   Item # 069067

What Works in Preventing Rural Violence
by Wilder Research Center

An in-depth review of eighty-eight effective strategies you can use to prevent and intervene in violent behaviors, improve services for victims, and reduce repeat offenses. This report also includes a Community Report Card with step-by-step directions on how you can collect, record, and use information about violence in your community.

94 pages, softcover   Item # 069040

ORDERING INFORMATION

Order by phone, fax or online

Call toll-free: 800-274-6024
Internationally: 651-659-6024

Fax: 651-642-2061

E-mail: books@wilder.org
Online: www.wilder.org/pubs

Mail: Amherst H. Wilder Foundation
Publishing Center
919 Lafond Avenue
St. Paul, MN 55104

Our NO-RISK guarantee

If you aren't completely satisfied with any book for
any reason, simply send it back within 30 days for
a full refund.

Pricing and discounts

For current prices and discounts, please visit our
web site at www.wilder.org/pubs or call toll free at
800-274-6024.

Do you have a book idea?

Wilder Publishing Center seeks manuscripts and
proposals for books in the fields of nonprofit management and community development. To get a copy of
our author guidelines, please call us at 800-274-6024.
You can also download them from our web site at
www.wilder.org/pubs/author_guide.html.

Visit us online

You'll find information about the Wilder Foundation
and more details on our books, such as table of con-
tents, pricing, discounts, endorsements, and more, at
www.wilder.org/pubs.

Quality assurance

We strive to make sure that all the books we publish
are helpful and easy to use. Our major workbooks are
tested and critiqued by experts before being published.
Their comments help shape the final book and—we
trust—make it more useful to you.